Selah †
Think about it!

EVANGELIST KING

Copyright © 2015 The Children's Mite. All rights reserved.

This book may not be copied or reprinted for commercial gain or profit. The use of short quotations, prayers or occasional page copying for personal or group bible study is permitted and encouraged.

Although every precaution has been taken to verify the accuracy of the information contained herein, the author and publisher assume no responsibility for any errors or omissions. No liability is assumed for damages that may result from the use of information contained within.

ISBN-13: 978-0692478547 (The Children's Mite)
ISBN-10: 069247854X

DEDICATION

To my Heavenly Father and LORD and Savior, Christ Jesus and the Holy Spirit. Without, I cannot do anything. Selah †

CONTENTS

Acknowledgement	i
Preface	1
Discipleship	2
Leadership	53
Parenthood	72
Relationships	78

ACKNOWLEDGEMENT

I want to thank my husband of 30 years. He encouraged me to do this book many years ago. I love you, Roger!

Shalom †

PREFACE

Selah is a Hebrew word meaning "to think on, to ponder or to meditate on" and can be found seventy-one times in the Psalms and three times in Habakkuk. Selah moments happen in our lives every day whether we notice them or not. Too often we as human beings find ourselves thinking about or meditating on the problems of the day which produces frustration, worry and fear which are completely opposite of what our Heavenly Father wants us to focus on, which is His Word. If what we think about and meditate on does not produce or build our faith in God, we need a change of focus — a change in what we are spending our Selah moments on.

What follows in this book is the result of Holy Spirit inspired comments that were posted on the social media Facebook profile of Evangelist King. The compilation of these Selah moments inspired by the LORD Christ Jesus through His Holy Spirit will not only bless, heal and inspire, but will also motivate and teach you simple truths found in God's Word that can be applied to EVERY situation in your life.

Before reading this book, pray against and bind demon spirit offense. For it will attack and cause you to take offense against what is said and written. Remember, God's powerful Word is sharp as a surgeon's scalpel, cutting through everything, whether doubt or defense, laying us open to listen and obey. Nothing and no one is impervious to God's Word. We can't get away from it—no matter what. It is quick to judge the inner reflections and attitudes of the heart.

May the LORD God speak to you as you Selah † Think about It!

DISCIPLESHIP

Demon spirit gossip is VERY effective on Facebook. All a person need to do is share it and hundreds (or thousands) of people are affected. Selah †

What TRULY needs to be defended? Is it THE FAITH or YOUR FAITH? Selah †

BEFORE my deliverance, I felt strange presences in my bedroom. Even though I didn't see anything, I knew something were there. Then I heard the Voice of the LORD say, "Terry, you have objects in your room that need to be thrown away." So He showed me those objects and my husband I cleaned our house spiritually. Now that was our house. About a month or two later, God directed me to my human helper because He wanted to clean His house. Those same demons were still living in His house which is my mind, will, emotions and body. As instructed, I obeyed and went to the woman of God and God cleaned His house. Therefore; dear hearts. You may get rid of evil objects out of your house; but when those same demons who are in those objects remain in you, your house will not stay spiritually clean because you're not spiritually cleaned. Firstly, allow the Holy Spirit to lead you to your human helper to throw out EVERY spirit not of Him and then your house will STAY spiritually clean. Selah †

It's not your house that's demonized, it's God's house (you). Selah †

Don't be so fast to agree with someone when they say, "God". They may not be referring to the God of Abraham, Isaac and Jacob. Selah †

SELAH † THINK ABOUT IT!

People (of God), regardless of how ministers have taught and preached about being pregnant and carrying your destiny in your womb and then say, push; if you feel something moving in your belly, that's not the Holy Spirit! Its spirit snake and you need to be delivered from it. This is the reason why so many children of God CANNOT enter into their destiny in Christ Jesus because spirit snake prevents them. Get delivered from that thing in Jesus' mighty name. Selah †

AFTER your deliverance, FALSE pastors, apostles, prophets, prophetesses, evangelists and teachers will NOT rejoice with you in being set TOTALLY free. Devils in them will discourage you and will speak evil about the one whom the LORD God used to set you free. RUN AWAY from such leaders. For they are NOT of and from God. Selah †

Do you not know that when you accuse a person of having a specific demon in them, you BEST know its TRUTH? IF not, that same demon will enter you. Selah †

Did Jesus bear arms? He told Peter to put away his weapons and said, if you live by it, you will die by it. Selah †

You do know that one can be always learning but never able to come to full knowledge of the truth? Selah †

When I receive a friend request from most people I know God's reason and it is they need deliverance from a spirit lover. The saddest part is they think they don't. Selah †

We often hear stories about people living in other parts of the world who are blatantly involved in witchcraft/ungodly covenant and how demons follow and talk to them and think it doesn't happen in the USA. Well, we need to THINK. Take a Selah moment! The people born and raised in the USA have ancestral roots from those countries. Therefore, they are STILL connected and demons know this truth. I just ministered to a woman who confessed that her father was a warlock and died two years ago. She's not from Africa and was born and raised in America. She stated that demons have been following her before her father died and they were trying to convince her to do as her father. They would even show up in her dreams. Spirit husband even suggested that she leave her hometown and move to another city in which she did and she is now sleeping in her vehicle. She knew she needed deliverance and wanted to serve the LORD God with all her heart. She had NEVER had deliverance since coming to the LORD while in prison. Dear Hearts, there are MANY people raised and born in America who are following ancestral spirits and don't even know it. These devils are telling them they are only going back to their roots; but what they don't know is that they're serving and accepting ancestral spirits. Dear Hearts, be careful when you feel led to go back to your roots (ex., African, Hebraic). Ask yourself? Were they bound to the LORD God, the devil, the law or themselves? Selah †

Women (of God). Selah (Think about it)! Before your deliverance, your wardrobe consisted of garments that were tight fitting on your body. Displaying every shape and curve. Do you not know who it was that suggested to buy such garments? It was spirit snake. Spirit snake works very close with spirit husband; and their aim, through you, is to KEEP a man (and women these days) bound to demon spirit lust as well as you. Now, after your deliverance, you are no longer control by spirit snake. Your clothing is no longer tight on your body. For you know the TRUE beauty of a woman is inwardly. Selah †

I know my daughter's Facebook friends get tired of seeing my posts on her Wall. Since the LORD God set her free from spirit lover (and friends), she is NOW able to enjoy and share the Word of God. Selah †

When God is about to set you TOTALLY free and you "feel" fearful, that is not you! The strongman know it's about to leave God's premises and it has called for reinforcement. Spirit fear will keep the door open for the strongman. Therefore; the next time God is about to DO something and you feel fearful, REMEMBER that is not you and go ahead and do what

SELAH † THINK ABOUT IT!

the LORD God instructed. Selah †

If you're around filthiness all day; it doesn't matter how much you try, the stench will get on you. LIKEWISE, when you're in the company of a person who is always speaking evil about another person OR if you have Facebook friends who are always sharing negativity about others and you share them with your friends, devils will get into you. Selah †

Since coming to the LORD in 1994, the church leaders I was raised around made it appear that Christ Jesus only worked with them. They were the ones who the LORD would use to save, heal and deliver those in need. So we, the lay members, depended on our leaders in doing so. BUT when I started searching the Scripture and reading for myself, I saw differently. I saw that signs, miracles, wonders and the dispelling of demons should always follow Believers in Christ Jesus wherever they go. I saw that it is not a special gift that God will give one person and not the other. I'm the type of person who believes in not only what I read, but also I will put to practice what I'm reading. So one day I tried it. I used the Name of Jesus and commanded devils to go and they went. One day I used the Name of Jesus and commanded sickness to leave and it went. We, as Believers, should be living a Godly lifestyle; and when we does, the evidence of our life in Christ Jesus will be salvation, healing, deliverance and giving. We're not any special than our Fellow Believers. Selah †

And you wonder why I'm so aggressive against the works of darkness. It's because devils will talk a person out of their healing, deliverance, giving and salvation. Selah †

Sometimes it's just BEST not to have church members as Facebook friends. Besides, it's only the sick that needs a physician. Selah †

People may not forgive and hold your past sins against you; but God, after repentance, says, "What sins?" Selah †

EVANGELIST KING

I love Africa; and if I relocated there and made my citizenship permanent, even though I may see things I don't agree with, I would not talk against Africa due to my love for Africa. If I hate what Africa does that much, then I would just move back to my own country. Selah †

Sometimes it is not demons that have a grip on a person. The person has a grip on the demons. So who need to release who? Disobedience to God keeps them tightly in your grip. Selah †

Wouldn't it be sad and disappointing to die and expect to enter the Kingdom of Heaven and the Angel of the LORD say, "You can't come here because you didn't LIKE such-and-such?" Selah †

When someone works in manure all day and every day, they don't even realize they stinks. LIKEWISE, whenever we for a long time fellowship with people who are causing confusion and division, a residue of stench will be on us and we'll not even realize it. As I once told this truth to a dear sister, she didn't believe it. But several months later, she called me for help. Immediately, I commanded that demon to come out and it manifested. She was set free once again. Therefore, you do know that you can "feel" good and still be demonized? Deliverance is needed in Jesus mighty name. Selah †

As the Apostle Paul let us know, he had a thorn in the flesh. You know, a thorn in the flesh is a nuisance. If not removed, it continues to buffer or poke at you. There was something that not all the time, but sometimes irritated the Apostle Paul and he wanted Christ Jesus to stop it by removing it. Jesus Christ would not and reminded Paul of His mercy and grace was all he needed. Dear Hearts, we as God's child as the Apostle Paul has a thorn that irritates our flesh. As for me, it seems like I been dealing with this same issue over and over again. Now, I realize today that it is my thorn in the flesh. You know, since coming to the LORD God and being a woman of God; and it only happens in the church, the men (most of the time the male leaders) when they want to know more about me, what I do or want me to know what I should not be doing; they don't come directly to me, but go to my husband and ask or tell him what they want me to know. 100% of the time the things they tell him to tell me does not build love in his heart toward me. They act as though I do not have a mouth to talk; but think since coming to my husband and not me, they have done it the biblical way. Once I was worshiping in church service and I was doing it quietly. I was in the Presence of God. So we went home and then I heard the LORD say, "Terry, the pastor didn't like it when you were standing up worshiping me. He's going to have his elder call Roger and tell him to tell you." I said, "Yes, LORD." Then I told Roger what the LORD had just said to me. Dear Hearts, it wasn't even two minutes after I told Roger that the phone rang. He answered and it was one of the elders of the church and he told Roger exactly as the LORD told me. We never attended that church again. Over the years, more things happened pertaining to this subject and even till now. Just as the LORD God told the Apostle Paul that his mercy and grace is sufficient; LIKEWISE, I look to his mercy and grace to keep this thorn in the flesh under control. People don't realize it, but women in God and working in the ministry goes through a more intense battle than men all because of people's misunderstanding of God's Word concerning women keeping silent in the church. Therefore; dear hearts, don't do as some. IF you want to know what I do and want me to know what I shouldn't be doing; don't go to my husband and tell him so he can tell me. Come directly to me. For this is the correct biblical way. Selah †

Even in human life, there MUST be balance in our diet in order to grow strong and healthy. LIKEWISE, in our spiritual life, we MUST have balance. It's good to go to ministries that believe in deliverance; but we must also KEEP balance in our lives. For its only through the teaching of God's Word that we'll receive the spiritual nutrients we need in order to grow and mature in the LORD. Improper diet will result in off balance and therefore cause retardation. LIKEWISE, spiritually. That is why we see so many people (of God) who are spiritual retarded. It's because they do not have a proper spiritual diet in their lives. In other words, they do not mediate and study the Word of God with the inner motive of living by EVERY Word that comes from His mouth. The teaching of God's Word is crucial for our survival in life. Again, deliverance is great; but in order to maintain our deliverance, we MUST be feed and eat the Word of God which is we MUST be taught God's Word in order to continue to grow strong and healthy in the LORD God. I love deliverance ministries; but most important, I love to hear the Word of God being taught. For faith ONLY comes as I hear the Word of God. Selah †

Christ Jesus doesn't see success the way we see success. That's why there will be MANY to say on that GREAT Day; "LORD, I have cast out demons in your name. I have healed the sick in your name. I have done miracles in your name." Selah †

When you're spiritually matured, you will not only respect and honor your man and/or woman of God; but God's man and woman of God. Selah †

As Satan spoke through the mouth of Peter without Peter realizing it. Recently I had a dear relative say to me, "Your mouth is going to get you into a lot of trouble." I then thought about it and SUDDENLY these words rose up through me, "Yes! In trouble with the devil and he can't do anything about it!" The person just looked at me in silence and anger. HALLELUJAH! Christ Jesus said He has given us ALL power and authority against Satan and his demons. Meaning, we are FREE to speak TRUTH without fearing what the devil (and mankind) wants to do to us. I have decided years ago to exercise my God-given rights in Christ Jesus to the fullest as He has allowed me. GLORY TO GOD!!!! Selah †

You know, there are some things we do and we'll be unable to blame the devil for it when we meet Christ Jesus. Some people never cease to amaze me. They request friendship only on Facebook and when I post what the LORD God has and is doing for and through me, they get offended. They get offended by what I place on my own Wall. It's like when someone comes to your house; and once inside, they get upset because of the way you decided to decorate your own house. What FOOLISHNESS! It just show us that deliverance is needed in the House of God. Selah †

REMEMBER, the LORD God says if we're ashamed of him in any shape,

SELAH † THINK ABOUT IT!

form or fashion, he'll be ashamed of us on that GREAT Day. Selah †

When you quote the Word of God, please be sure to explain the Word of God. MANY people can quote Scripture, but they cannot teach the Scripture. Understanding is the most importance of our getting. It will eliminate a lot of problems. Selah †

When you look at a person, what is the FIRST thing you see? Is it their flaw? Know that is not what Jesus Christ sees when He looks at us? Selah †

Will we ever learn that our battles and REAL enemies are not with flesh and blood whom we can see with our human eyes? And we call ourselves spiritual. Selah †

Wearing a prayer shawl doesn't make you any holier or righteous. Remember, Judas also wore one. Selah †

The gifts of the Holy Spirit are not "your" gifts. They are His manifestations; and He choose who He wills to manifest through. Selah †

Jesus Christ healed 10 lepers and only one returned to give Him thanks. LIKEWISE, there are MANY the LORD God freed from demonic bondage and blessed through you and there will be only a few to give you credit in doing so. Selah †

God used the female vessel to anoint and/or set free MANY great men of God. Don't under estimate the power of God through a woman. KEEP your eyes on God and not the vessel. Shalom and Selah †

The proof of desire is in the pursuit. What are you pursuing? Is it God? Is it a wife? Is it a husband? Is it things? Your pursuit determines your happiness. Therefore, choose wisely. Selah †

Since doing deliverance sessions, I have observed in the USA that the people living in certain states (Florida, Georgia, Maryland, North Carolina, South Carolina, Virginia, West Virginia, Delaware, Alabama, Kentucky, Mississippi, Tennessee, Arkansas, Louisiana, Oklahoma and Texas) are deeper into sexual bondage and witchcraft than people living in other states. Demons are territorial. Selah †

We need to realize that it is Jesus, the Christ, who chooses the vessel in which He heals and/or delivers us through. There have been many who have gone to SCOAN and was not healed and/or delivered. It was because SCOAN was not the vessel in which He chosen to heal or deliver them through. I spoke to many people who had visited SCOAN and was not healed or delivered; and when I prayed for them, they were healed and/or delivered. Dear Hearts, our hearts should always be opened to hear the Voice of God in leading us to our helper here on earth. Selah †

I was first labeled "a witch" in 1995 and it hurt my feelings so bad that I went to the LORD crying. As I cried, He said, "Terry, they called me a warlock. If they said it about Me, they will say it about those who follow me. Is the servant greater that their Master?" I stopped crying and said, "Yes, LORD." Dear Hearts, it doesn't matter what you may think of me. All that matters to me is what the LORD God thinks of me. He's the ONLY One who can destroy body and spirit. Selah †

Burning incense for comfort and/or protection is witchcraft and deliverance is needed in Jesus' mighty name. The Holy Spirit is our ONLY Comforter and Protector. Selah †

Most people get excited when they get a new house, car or a new job. I'm happy to have those things, but they don't give me excitement. I TRULY get excited when the LORD God connect me to His child or children. Now,

SELAH † THINK ABOUT IT!

that excites me! Selah †

Do you not know that some people cell phone is Satan's property? The person uses it to do all KINDS of evil works on and from it. Therefore, demons are attached to it. Be careful! You don't want to buy such phones! And you wonder why all of a sudden you're lusting. Selah †

I do not believe in cursing my enemies because our LORD God told us not to curse our enemies. Therefore, I don't pray such prayers either. Selah †

Remember, no fornicator shall inherit the Kingdom of God. Selah †

If you're smoking cigarettes, sniffing snuff or doing SUCH LIKE; you will not enter the Kingdom of God. For these things are not found in The Kingdom. Repent and sin no more! Then get that devil thrown out of the house (mind, will, emotions, body) in Jesus' mighty name. Selah †

Sometimes demons are talking to you through a person and you don't even know and you say, "I have discernment." Discernment based on your knowledge? We need the Gift of Discerning of Spirits which is based on the Holy Spirit's knowing and then we will discern or see ALL types of spirits as the Holy Spirit wills. Selah †

As I was reading over my first self- published book I done in 1995 for corrections, I realized why Satan tried so hard to discourage me in the beginning. I truly see, which I did not see then, Satan was afraid of what I will become in the future. Praise God! He did not allow me to give up! All praise goes to Christ Jesus! Selah †

If my LORD Jesus Christ of Nazareth was accused of being a warlock, then why should I be troubled when accused of being a witch? I did challenge my accusers to a Holy Ghost Showdown, but they never responded. Selah †

If you're ashamed of the LORD in any way, He's going to be ashamed of you before His Father on that Great Day and the most subtle way of being ashamed of Him is being ashamed of His servant. Who are we to even think of being ashamed to be with or around someone? Jesus isn't ashamed of us. He sees and hears us and comes to our rescue and fellowship with us when we call on His name and He acts through His servants. Selah †

A woman asked a question in a deliverance group. Her job insisted all employees undergo hypnotism. She refused and told them why. They asked her to show them the Scripture that says it is wrong. So she asked for a Scripture. As I was reading the comments, I noticed that nobody gave her a Scripture; but continued to explain why it is wrong. Then I heard the LORD God say, "Tell her to go to this Scripture because it's included." So I informed her to go to Galatians 5:19-21 and wrote, "It's included in the saying...AND SUCH LIKE..." Therefore, dear hearts, the next time someone says to show them in the Bible where it's wrong to do a certain thing and the Scripture do not list that particular thing, just tell them, "AND SUCH LIKE". God is so GOOD! Selah †

It has been said, "You're so heavenly minded, you're no earthly good." But I say to you, "Be heavenly minded and you're be no earthly good to the devil." Selah †

If you were part of a false church and you left; but due to that experience, you no longer desire to attend any church, it means that you're still connected to the "root" of that false church and deliverance is needed in Jesus' mighty name. Selah †

Before the LORD delivered me from a demon lurking in my mind, will, emotions and body; I would look up to some men and women of God and look down at others. After He delivered me, I observed I no longer did

SELAH † THINK ABOUT IT!

that; and Jesus spoke to me and said, "Terry, the problem was in you and not my servant." Selah †

Any involvement in the occult will get you demonized. Whether a person played the Ouija board or such like need more than just prayer. The demons in them need to be confronted and commanded out the house! There need to be a confrontation in Jesus' mighty name. Selah †

When God set you free, it changes you from the inside and reflects outward. He's AWESOME! Selah †

It won't be water, but fire next time. Selah †

God is a God of excellence! Which means; whatever state you're in, give Him your best. Don't concern yourself with what others have or how others look. You give Him your best. That's what matters to God. Selah †

It just amazes me when a person has respect for their man or woman of God, but don't have respect for God's man or woman of God. Selah †

Spirit Leviathan is a strong-willed demon. Its main responsibility is to get a person to not believe in deliverance or to believe they don't need deliverance. It's arrogant and will boastfully say, "I don't need deliverance. I know all about deliverance. I have been in deliverance ministry for such-and such years." It does not and will not humbly itself to say as King David, "LORD, search my heart. IF there be any darkness in me, take it out of me." Spirit Leviathan is also two-headed. One head appears to be submissive when in the presence of people; while the other head is full of anger and rage. By being two headed, it's double-minded. Beware of spirit Leviathan. Selah †

Spirit Jezebel is not sexual lust. It is a demon spirit against Godly authority that works with spirit lust and spirit snake. Just because you see a woman (or man) that looks sexy does not mean that is spirit Jezebel. It is spirit snake. Spirit snake and spirit lust are demons that entices females and males to focus on their sexuality and spirit Jezebel uses snake and lust to open the door for it. Be careful! Don't be observing yourself as "sexy"! You'll receive what you don't want — spirit Jezebel and friends! See yourself as the LORD God see you — as His creation beautiful and wonderfully made in His image and likeness. Selah †

There are MANY people using Facebook as their podium to teach and/or preach what they want to say and to be heard because they are forbidden by their leader to do so in their local assembly. They are angry and upset with the local church to the point they have forsaken or given up on attending church. There also are those who still attend their local church, but angry. Anger against authority for any reason will open a door for spirit Jezebel. Therefore, on Facebook; some people will pick and choose their audience of friends and spirit Jezebel will have them to reject the friendship of TRUE men and women of God by removing and/or blocking them. BEWARE of spirit Jezebel on Facebook! Selah †

When you TRULY understand Godly authority, then it doesn't matter who God uses to empower His authority through. You will submit to that authority because it's God. IF you have a problem submitting to Godly authority whenever it comes through a vessel of God's choice that is spirit Jezebel. It doesn't matter whether you're an apostle, prophet, evangelist, pastor or teacher; whenever an anointed and appointed vessel who God has chosen to be the lead and you doesn't submit to God's authority through them, then spirit Jezebel is alive and well in you. For this is what it truly mean when Scripture says, the spirit of the prophet is subject to the prophet. You'll be surprised to know there are MANY apostles and prophets (prophetesses) with spirit Jezebel. Selah †

Seeing the dead is not a gift from God. Selah †

Sometimes I may see video clips of a demonized person. To me it's not

SELAH † THINK ABOUT IT!

funny to see demons use human bodies for their glory. I don't know which is the saddest-the demonized person or the person that claims to be a Christian and think the video is funny. Selah †

Suspicion is not love and certainly not the leading of Holy Ghost. We, as dear children of God, don't need to be suspicious of one another. It's sad whenever I reach out to my brother or sister in Christ and they are suspicious of me. We live in a selfish world; and if we're not careful, we'll become selfish, too. We will think, "This person want something from me." There's nothing no one in this world can give me that satisfies my soul. It is ONLY the Holy Spirit Who can do that. Christ Jesus has commissioned us to love one another and when you love a person, you'll show it at least by communicating with them. In America, there are diversities of people and that is a blessing. We, as God's dear children, is not concern with differences-rather its race or culture. Therefore, whenever I meet a person, I TRULY don't allow race or culture to affect my friendship or communication. I will talk to you as though I've known you all my life. I have found that most Christians are uncomfortable whenever I do that and that is so sad. It shows me there's something within that need to be destroyed in Jesus' mighty name. I have God and my husband to thank for changing me. Before meeting my husband, I ONLY was around Black people and I was raised only around Black people. But when I became grown and met Roger that changed because he was brought up around different nationalities. He always impressed me whenever we would go out in how he cheerfully communicated with all people. It didn't matter to him what your race or culture were. Watching him helped me to come out of my shell and meeting Christ Jesus empowered me not to see race or culture, but to see them as His dear children. Dear Hearts, let's stop being suspicious of one another and see people as Christ Jesus see them. Selah †

You will actually be surprised to know that some church buildings are demon possessed. Therefore; during service time, you know what manner of spirit rules. Selah †

Demons will say the name Jesus because there is a false Jesus. Don't be

EVANGELIST KING

fooled! Selah †

Devils tremble and cringe at the voice of an anointed servant of God. It burst their ear drums and the human person then place their finger in their ears. Deliverance is needed in Jesus' mighty name for the human agent. Selah †

It's okay to shout out loud at baseball or basketball games; but not in church festivities. The devil is a liar--all day long! Selah †

The devil hates Holy Ghost FIRE! He says, "You're too loud." Selah †When I was a little girl and read where Jesus said if you live by the sword, you will die by the sword; it put Godly fear in me. I decided then to let Jesus deal with vengeance. Selah †

REMEMBER, for EVERY 850 false prophets, there will be one true prophet. Selah †

A religious spirit says "Show me Scripture" with intentions of never to obey. Selah †

I once heard a true story of a man plucking out his eye because he read the Scripture that said, if your left eye offend you, pluck it out. It just shows, we need the Holy Spirit to reveal TRUTH to us when we read Scripture. For the letter kills, but the Spirit gives life. The Pharisees and Sadducees hated Jesus because they only went by the letter of the Law. That religious spirit is still in operation today. Selah †

I'm only commissioned to speak TRUTH, not to force you to DO TRUTH. Selah †

SELAH † THINK ABOUT IT!

If I ask you to share with me when you first gave your life to Christ Jesus and you cannot, it means deliverance is needed in Jesus' mighty name. Selah †

The first time I heard the Word of God being taught on a specific topic and then demonstrated by the Holy Ghost was through Pastor Bob Larson. Before that, I only heard ministers talk and no action. If you speak on healing, then afterward stretch out your hand and touch those who need healing. If you speak on deliverance, then stretch out your hand and touch those who need deliverance. If you speak on prophecy, then stretch out your hand to save, heal and deliver those in need. Don't just be a talker. Add action to your faith. The Holy Ghost desire to manifest the goodness of God through the Sons of God. Selah †

As Holy Spirit lead, when I personally meet a woman (of God) that shows off her cleavage, I don't walk away and talk about her. I pull her aside and share lovingly with her why she should not dress in such manner. Some, if not most women, doesn't know it is spirit snake who suggest that they should dress this way. Such women need deliverance and is not even aware of it. When the woman get right with God, then she can CLEARLY see how to get the men right with God (example: the Samaritan woman at the well). Selah †

One day as I was scrolling my News Feed looking at posts and comments, the LORD said, "Most people are on Facebook to be heard instead of hearing." Selah †

Some words of wisdom Jesus did not share with others. He shared only with His disciples. LIKEWISE, there are times I will not go into depth understanding on the posts I may share. Not everyone who follow me, follow to be a disciple of Jesus Christ. This is why I will seldom extend the invitation to speak directly to and with you instead of writing lengthy conversations. Some things cannot be written. It BEST to be spoken. Selah †

EVANGELIST KING

You can lead a horse to the water, but you can't make it drink. A young woman from London sent me a message asking if she could speak to me. I scheduled a time for us to speak. She then began to tell me her specific problem. I ministered truth to her. Then SUDDENLY I asked, "Do you wear wigs?" She replied, "Yes." I then shared what the LORD wanted me to tell her. After I finished, I said, "The LORD had been telling you not to wear wigs. This isn't the first time you have heard this." She replied, "Yes. I'm going to throw them all out today." Dear Hearts, it's crucial that we OBEY the LORD's instructions. When He tells us to DO something, you best believe it's for our good. Selah †

Whatever you say you do for the LORD, He looks in the heart for an inner motive. Judas made it appear his heart was for the poor-those in financial need. TRUTHFULLY, it was not. It was for himself. His heart was full of creed. Judas thought the perfume that was used to anoint Jesus' body was a waste and could have been used to help the poor. Judas wasn't concern for the poor. He was concern for himself. We may fool somebody, but we can't fool everybody. Selah †

It's sad to read comments where those who lack KNOWING the works of Holy Spirit vs the works of Satan. No wonder the LORD says at that Day, many will come and say they did such-and-such in His name and He will command them to leave Him because He never knew them. No relationship - No KNOWING your Father's Voice - His Word. Selah †

When I was a young girl I loved to sit and listen to my Grandmother tell stories about her experiences. This one particular experience she shared, I would listen and was in awe as she told it. She told that same story to me and others for over 30 years and each time I was in awe. When I accepted Jesus Christ into my life, I began to KNOW His TRUTH. So one day I was over her house and she told that same story again; but this time, I was listening with my spiritual ears instead of my physical ears. After she finished, I looked at her and said, "Grandma! That was not your twin sister that came to you! That was demon spirit death!" She got quiet and never repeated that story to me again. Dear Hearts, again; your dead loved ones are not coming to you physically or in the dream. Its demon

SELAH † THINK ABOUT IT!

spirit death and it wants you next! Selah †

You CANNOT work for a company with an inner motive of solely building your own repertoire. This is UNFAITHFULNESS; and anything built on unfaithfulness will not stand. Selah †

I TRULY see why the LORD God CANNOT use some people. As King Saul, they don't follow specific instructions, but do it the way they want it to be done. Such people would not make good leaders. Selah †

When I rejected God in my life, I lived in constant fear. I feared going to hell because I knew I was rejecting Him. I feared going to sleep because I would dream of sinking in a deep dark hole. I didn't have any peace of mind. This continued to happen until I finally accepted Jesus Christ in my heart and life. Those fears went away. I say that to say this. Your fear of going to hell or you will not be saved is caused by your rejection of God in your life. It is demon spirit fear who is actually whispering lies in your hearing that you're going to hell because it knows as long as you reject Christ Jesus in your life that is where you will be going if you died. Perfect LOVE, who is Christ Jesus, cast out fear. Accept Him into your life today. Kneel down on your knees and say, "LORD Jesus, forgive me for ALL my sins or wrongdoings. Forgive me for rejecting You. LORD Jesus, come into my heart and live your PERFECT life in and through me. Baptize me in Your Precious Blood. Save me, heal me and deliver me from ALL unrighteousness. This I ask by and in faith. In Jesus' mighty name. Amen." Now, IF you asked God in faith to save, heal and deliver you, then go to our website at http://www.thechildrensmite.org/contactus and submit the Deliverance Request Submission Form. Please indicate in the MESSAGE section that you accepted Jesus Christ as your LORD and Savior through this book, I will give immediate attention to your request. Selah †

After a deliverance session, the LORD God led me to say to the person, "Those demons are going back to the man and woman who tried to curse you through witchcraft and say, "It didn't work! Now, we're going to beat you up!" It took a few seconds for the person to register what I had said. Then we laughed. Dear Hearts, you can't curse who God has blessed and you sure can't bless who God has cursed. Selah †

I'm reminded of a time when my husband and I were attending this church MANY years ago. As I began to worship the LORD during the Worship Service, the LORD told me to ONLY focus on Him and tune distractions out. So I did. As I was worshiping Him with my hands outstretched to Him, I heard a bug buzzing around my head. I ignored it and continued to worship the LORD with ALL my heart. The bug flew closer and hit me on my lip. With my eyes still closed, I swung my right hand and continued to worship the LORD. The buzzing stopped. We returned home and I prepared for bed. I took off my blouse and then my bra. When I took off my bra, I yelled and hit my breast. I then looked at what I had hit off my breast. I thought I was seeing things and looked at it several times. It was a burnt cock roach. I asked how did it get inside my bra and where did it come from? The LORD then told me. He said it was witchcraft. As I was worshiping Him, a lady who did not like me sent curses at me. He told me the buzzing sound I heard was witchcraft sent at me; but His Presence- His FIRE POWER- burned it. He allowed it to manifest as a burnt cock roach so that I may know what was going on. PRAISE GOD! About a few months later, the woman who I did not even know, found my home phone number somehow and called me. When I answered the phone, she was trembling in fear. Every word she spoke was uttered in fear and she asked if I would forgive her because she just did not like me. Of course, unsure of who she was, I forgave her. She then hung up the phone. To this day, I still don't know who that lady was. I thank God for EVERY spiritual experience He has given me. Selah †

It TRULY saddens my heart to know that the LORD God delivered His child from demonic oppression and they turned their back on Him by yielding to temptation and acting like nothing happened. He knows and so does His servant. Selah †

Frankly, I'm happy that I don't hold verbal conversations with most people. That way when Holy Spirit lead me to post His TRUTH, you can't say I'm throwing stones and it will be true. Selah †

It is said, "Great lions hunt alone." I watch Nat Geo all the time whenever it is about lions. I have observed a lion hunting alone and the result ended in death to the great lion. You see, the male lion actually need the female lions in order to survive. Without them, they will starve. So I think that phrase, "Great lions hunt alone" should be rethought. Selah †

Spirit spouse is a trickster! The very moment you decide to contact the man or woman of God for deliverance that spirit will get quiet in your life. They do this to trick you in 'thinking' that they are no longer there. Therefore, there's no need to contact the man or woman of God. You will experience 'feeling' good and this feeling is your evidence that you are indeed free. THIS IS A LIE FROM THE MASTER LIAR!!! Our evidence of FREEDOM is not in our feelings! When you succumb to this feeling and made up your mind in not contacting the man or woman of God, it is then when the spirit spouse comes out of its quietness and cause mishaps in your life. Then you will equate those mishaps to God teaching you a lesson in having trust in Him when God didn't have anything to do with those mishaps. You will not experience TOTAL freedom in mind, will, emotions and body as long as spirit spouse (and friends) remain in the house. They MUST be evicted and thrown out by God's anointed and appointed servant in Jesus' mighty name. Selah †

I wish you could have heard the conversation I had with a woman who lives in The Netherlands who contacted me for deliverance from witchcraft. She is from Suriname. Her family's lineage is steep into witchcraft. Her brother is a well-known witch doctor in Suriname and on YouTube. She also dabbed her hand into the craft. She began to share with me how spirit husband which is known by another name in Suriname is a trickster. She knew names of MANY demons in the Marine Kingdom because she use to be part of that darkness which they call heaviness. She shared with me how python works in their country of Suriname which was the very same way the LORD God revealed to me. It was amazing to hear her talk about these things as they are known in their country because I have been saying the exact same thing but in different terminology. I told her to THANK God because if He had not led her to His anointed and appointed servant, whenever she began to talk about these things, the person would have ran in fear. She was set TOTALLY free in Jesus' mighty name. Selah †

People may look good on the outside; but inwardly, they need deliverance. Selah †

I went back and listened to the audio of a deliverance session. When I started the FIRE prayers, the demons blanked the person out and she did not hear any of the FIRE prayers. As I was listening to the recording, I noticed the sounds I heard in the session were not recorded on the recording. That spirit snake hissed at me several times and spirit husband was right there with it. I heard these sounds, but they were not recorded on the recording. God is AWESOME! He does whatever He desire through His Spirit. It just shows us that we should NEVER go by what we see, hear or even feel as our evidence that the LORD has set us free. We RECEIVE ONLY by FAITH because what we TRULY bind or loose on earth, the LORD loose and binds in the heavens. Selah †

Never take Satan head on. Instead say, "The LORD rebuke you!" Selah †In order for devils to die (or cease its operations) in your life, you must not give them space to reign. Merely saying, "Die! Die! Die!" will not work IF you're giving them space in your life. Selah †

BEWARE women (of God) of bringing attraction to yourself. You just may get the attraction you don't want. Let the attraction of your heart's desire be of Christ Jesus so men will see Christ, the hope of Glory, shining BRIGHTLY through and on you. Selah †

Body piercings, including tribal piercings, carries an ungodly covenant. It symbolizes defiance. Defiance against the One Who made us and mockery against Jesus Christ. Jesus' body was pierced or mutilated for our transgressions. Our chastisement was upon Him. Therefore, there's

SELAH † THINK ABOUT IT!

no need for us to pierce or mutilate our body. The rings that are worn binds or secures that covenant. As a child of God, loose yourself from that evil covenant by repenting, removing and discarding the rings in Jesus' mighty name. Selah †

It's amazing, as sinners, how one can be VERY bold and unashamed of their deeds; but when they come to the LORD God, they seems to be timid and ashamed of the goodness of God. Selah †

In other words, Jesus says if we are ashamed of Him before mankind, He will be ashamed of us before His Father. I TRULY see more and more the demon spirit shame working among the children of God. This should not be. Selah †

BEWARE of making your requests known to the LORD out loud. REMEMBER, devils are looking and listening to EVERY word that comes out of your mouth. Their aim is to intercept your requests. It's BEST to pray in the Spirit and/or pray silently to yourself. After all, the devil can't read your mind; but he can read your lips. REMEMBER, only God can read your heart's desire. Instead, let the devil hear you PRAISING AND WORSHIPING THE LORD OUT LOUD. For this is something he hate to see and hear. Selah †

A TRUE prophetic word will bring deliverance. Selah †

TRUE evangelists will get less invitations to church events. For their aim is the salvation of souls and setting captives FREE; and in the local churches, folks 'think' they're already saved and free from demons within. Selah †

Jesus upon this earth did not encourage civil disobedience nor civil disrespect. We, as the children of God, does the same. Therefore, don't encourage it by sharing it. Selah †

Men, those of you who are striving to live holy before God, you cannot accept and connect with EVERY female who request Friendship on Facebook. It doesn't matter if they call themselves an apostle, prophetess, pastor or Christian. Most of these women on Facebook who have labeled themselves Christians, apostles, prophetesses or pastors are NOT truly seeking to serve the LORD with all their heart. Browse down their wall and you will see mostly selfies. This is demon spirit snake. Whenever you accept their request on Facebook, you automatically become connected to it. Some of these women who send requests, you plainly see they are not right; but yet, you think you're so strong in the LORD, you can handle it. You need to do as Joseph, but in this case, don't accept their request. When you accept their request, your light in the LORD will GRADUALLY grow dim and then you wonder why you're being tormented. Selah †

I have shared my testimony MANY times and as Apostle Paul, it's worth repeating and will ALWAYS be. Before the LORD God delivered me from inner demons, if someone would have told me they were in me, I would have called them a liar. After all, I loved the LORD with ALL my heart and He had forgiven me of ALL my sins. God doesn't look at us the way others may look at us or as we look at ourselves. When God look on or at us, He see right through us. I THANK Him for this quality because He could have left me the way I was, but He didn't. This is His mercy and grace. The LORD knew me and my ways, so He put it in my husband's heart to mention to me about a women's prayer breakfast that was held every Saturday morning. One morning the LORD instructed me to go. He did not explain the reason for going. He just said go and gave me specific instructions in what to do when I got there. At prayer breakfast, most likely, everyone's aim is to eat. But the LORD told me not to eat and when worship starts for me to stand and hold my hands up to worship Him and He was going to send the woman of God to me so she could lay her hands upon me. The LORD gave these specific instructions because He knew I don't allow everybody to lay their hands on me. So I obeyed the LORD's instructions. As I stood there worshiping the LORD, indeed the woman of God came over and laid her hands upon me and began to speak. As she was speaking, I heard Jesus speaking through her. As I was listening to Jesus, it was as though something was blocking me from clearly hearing Him. I was hoping Jesus would speak louder, but He would not. I strained my ears trying to hear Him, but something again kept blocking me from hearing Him. My desire to hear Him was strong and then SUDDENLY, I saw (and my eyes were closed) the woman of God placing her hand a few inches from my stomach and when she did, something came to attention. She began to move her hands upward very slowly and something in my belly was moving along with her hand. When her hand stopped, then something would stop. She started back moving her hand and something started moving along with her hand. Her hand came to my mouth and she said, there it goes! When she said those words, something flew out of my mouth. IMMEDIATELY my spirit began to say THANK YOU, JESUS. My mind was wondering why my spirit was saying thank you Jesus. My spirit knew exactly what had just happened, when my mind was clueless. Upon returning home, I went to the room where I usually mediate upon the LORD and these things were brought to my remembrance. So I asked the LORD what was that that flew out of my mouth. He said a demon. I was shocked! I asked Him how a demon got inside me. He told me and then I repented. Dear Hearts, when we sin against the LORD and repent, He will forgive us; but one thing you should know is that a demon might have come along with that disobedience. Therefore, it's best to allow Holy Spirit to lead you to His chosen and anointed servant in casting out that strong man. Selah †

The LORD says, "Be it according to your faith." Therefore, IF your faith is in going to Africa in order to be delivered, then go. Just be aware, the same God Who delivers in Africa will deliver right where you are. Selah †

Too often we look for an outward manifestation of demons as proof that we (or a person) has been set free. This is where we have made a BIG mistake because anything received of and by God is received by faith and not by sight or feelings. Just because you did not see (or feel) an outward manifestation when delivered from demons doesn't mean they did not leave. REMEMBER, it's up to Holy Spirit rather He choose to allow demons to make their presence or exit known and for His reason. Your part is to believe, receive and walk by FAITH in God's Word because He died for your FREEDOM! Selah †

Women (of God) don't fall prey to these men posing as pastors from Nigeria (or any other country). Satan hears you when you say out loud to the LORD that you want a Godly husband and he will send you a look-a-like. The man will appear to be EVERYTHING you have been looking for; not knowing he is actually a witchcraft worker in shepherd's clothing. Again, God don't work using a veil any longer and Facebook serves as one. The veil was torn when Jesus Christ gave His life for us. BEWARE and BE WARNED in Jesus' mighty name. Selah †

REMEMBER, Jesus done many things when He walked the earth that was not written in Scripture because the Book couldn't contain. The Holy Spirit reveals to us the mind of God and the tactics of the Enemy. When Jesus said there was no such thing as gender and marriage in the spirit realm, He knew something that we didn't know. He knew there were demons who say and do contrary to what God says and does. He knew there were demons who seek to have sexual intercourse with human beings-rather in the dream or in physical form. He knew these demons considered themselves to be the spiritual spouse of human beings even though God said there were no such thing as marriage and gender in the spirit realm. Sometimes we 'think' we know truth; when in truth, we don't know what we should know. Selah †

Due to Satan knowing his time will soon come to an end, he is strongly fighting against the Saints on earth so people can remain in captivity. This is the reason God's Word tell us to encourage one another in the faith. Saints on earth who are making an impact for the Kingdom of God comes under more spiritual attacks than those who are not making an impact. I received a message from a Brother in another country whose bookstore was shut down by the government due to him making known a prophetic book written by a powerful man of God. Even the cover of the book frightened the devil. The Holy Spirit, through His servant Apostle Paul, told us to STAND firm in our faith. No matter what may come or go, we are to STAND. Let us keep ALL the Saints of God on earth in prayer and encourage them. Selah †

SELAH † THINK ABOUT IT!

Be very selective who you send a Facebook friend request to when it comes. Better yet, show your spouse the person you're planning on requesting. Get their input. They just may save you from a headache. Selah †

I see that people want to be "propheLIED" to. No, can't do in my ministry. Selah †When you hear a person say that they went to such-and-such for deliverance and they could not deliver them, it is that demon who is actually doing the bragging. The cause is either or both. 1) You went to a person who is TRULY not God's anointed and chosen servant or 2) you lack faith in God. For the LORD says be it according to your own faith. Selah †

Seriously! You can't curse who God has blessed. Trying to curse who God has blessed will cause a curse to come upon you. For the LORD says, "I will bless who bless you and I will curse who curse you." Selah †

There is no revival without deliverance. Get delivered and you will be revived to be a revival. Selah †

A person can be bound in prison and then released. It's up to the person to do what the law instructs in order to remain free. LIKEWISE, our deliverance in Christ Jesus. Selah †

I usually don't have deliverance sessions past 5 pm (EST), but I made an exception for a young man schooling in India. It's GREAT when those seeking God for deliverance from demonic bondage within come with a humble spirit. The young man is from DR Congo-Zambia border and was saved in 2009, but he never upon receiving Christ gone through deliverance where the anointed and chosen servant of God commanded demon spirits to come out of his mind, will, emotions and body. Therefore, since 2009, he has been suffering from depression, spirits of death, confusion, uncontrollable lust, whoredom, spiritual wives and more. As I explained the reason why he suffered with such inner demons, he

CLEARLY saw the reason why. He confessed that his family indeed were involved in an ungodly covenant of idolatry and witchcraft. As I prayed for him and commanded evil spirits out of his mind, will, emotions and body, he felt something move in his private parts. I assured him it is the FIRE POWER OF THE HOLY GHOST setting ablaze EVERY spirit not of Him. After the session, he confessed to feeling lighter and he had such a bright glow on his face. Our session was through Google Hangouts and then Skype video. Now, I pray that he does not allow the evil ones to cause him to recant his testimony of the Goodness of God. As Jesus ALWAYS told them who he delivered, I told him, "Go and tell what great things God has done for you because somebody need to hear your testimony so they can be set free, too." Selah †

Once a so-called prophet invited my husband and me to minister with him in Georgia at a tent revival. On the second night he called on me to pray. So I prayed and began my prayer with "Our Father". I then heard the Holy Spirit through me praying. He asked for 10,000 angels to surround us. As I prayed like this, I could feel the so-called prophet looking at me in anger. I ignored him and continued to allow the Holy Spirit to pray through me. After the prayer, we heard gun shots. Unknowing what was happening, we continued the tent revival. The next morning we were told in the very same spot where we held revival, people were fatally shot. I then knew why the Holy Spirit asked for those angels to surround us. And by the way, the so-called prophet never asked me to pray again. Selah †

In the beginning of my walk with the LORD, an opportunity was given to me to minister to some young ladies for two days. On the first day, EVERYTHING turned out GREAT. The women listened intensely and was edified. I was ready for the second day. On the second day, the ladies returned and there was a new lady. Before I began the lesson, the new lady began to speak. What she was saying was true so I allowed her to continue and listened. I noticed she took the attention of the other ladies. She also had my attention. It went on for about 20 minutes. I was enjoying what she said and thought there was nothing wrong with allowing her to proceed. Then SUDDENLY, a voice thundered inside me and said, "You need to take control!" I shook and then took my hands and clapped them together. When I did, it made a thunderous sound and the lady suddenly stopped and came to attention. It was then that I realized that demon spirit in her had taken over the meeting and had distracted the other women from hearing TRUTH. I then began to teach. Dear Hearts, unless the LORD God tell us, we will not know when Satan creep in. Selah †

Be careful when people say you should be in agreement with them. Nowhere in Scriptures does it say for us to be in agreement DIRECTLY with one another. It is through the Word of God we should be in agreement with. A pastor's wife got up and made comment that two cannot walk together unless they agree. Stating that she do not want anybody around her that is not in agreement with her. This woman had a spirit husband in her because the LORD showed me. Just think when other women come in agreement with her, they too will receive that spirit husband. No, we are only to come in agreement with the Word of God and then through the Word we are in agreement and then we can walk together in unity of the Holy Spirit. Selah †

When it comes to casting demons out of people, you BEST depend upon the leadership of Holy Spirit. Depending upon the instructions of mankind will get you beat up as the sons of Sceva. Selah †

I remember the very first time I literally saw someone WALKING IN THEIR AUTHORITY. The servant of God just looked at the demon in the spirit realm in the young girl and raised his finger at it and the demon left. I was in AWE. The servant did not verbally speak out one word, but he walked in his authority. The demon knew authority when the people around God's servant did not. Now, that's where Jesus Christ wants to take us. Hallelujah! This is why at times during deliverance sessions you may or may not hear me say EXACTLY what you 'think' I should say. Selah †

Unbelief is one of the devil's goods. Selah †Once a person give their permission and give devils back their goods, the servant of God has FULL authority in dispelling them. But you can't give your permission and hold onto their goods thinking you can be set free of them. They have legal rights to their goods. Selah †

IF you're no threat to Satan; don't worry, he won't bother you. Selah †When it comes to knowledge, its good having it; but having it coupled with hands-on experience is even better. I'm not the type that just talk about what or how Christ Jesus heals and delivers. I also like to demonstrate what He demonstrated by the FIRE Power of the Holy Ghost. I never liked all talk, but no action. Of course, that's my personality the LORD has given to me. Selah †

When demons are in a person's mind, will, emotions and/or body and the person seek deliverance from God through His anointed and chosen servant, they will retaliate and strongly attack the person for connecting with God's servant. I have received MANY testimonies where demons tormented the person worse as they visited our website and considered submitting the request form. And the torment is even greater after they get delivered because those demons want to return to their house, they say. But GREATER is the Holy Spirit Who is in us than any devil in the world! Hallelujah! Selah †

Facebook is not my shield! Faith is! Selah †Spirit Jezebel seeks to silence TRUTH! Don't give in! God is calling us to repentance and spirit Jezebel don't want us to repent. Don't silence TRUTH. Selah †

Most people 'think' I discuss EVERYTHING with my husband, but I don't. I'm very selective in what I discuss with him because with him being a prophet, I want to hear God through him and not him telling me what I told him. Selah †

SELAH † THINK ABOUT IT!

It's sad due to the actions of so-called brothers and/or sisters in Christ Jesus, you have to add certain statements to protect yourself as an organization and/or ministry. Several years ago due to a person with spirit Jezebel, I had to add a warning on our deliverance sessions; and today, I had to add another warning to the reception of donations. Dear Hearts, it's not sinners you'll have the most problem(s) from. It's those who say they are in Christ Jesus. Selah †

I will take the wisdom and knowledge God has given me these MANY years and use them for His Glory. Again, nobody's mad, but the devil (and Jezebel). Selah †

The BIGGEST mistake one makes when they are dealing with a fatal sickness is to post about it on social media — not ALL of those on social media are TRULY your friend. My advice is to ONLY select those friends who are FULL of faith and the Holy Ghost to share it with so that they can fervently pray for you. It's only the fervent prayers of the righteous that God hears. Selah †

Spirit Jezebel choose its victim. It will use males, but its favorite victims are females. Females who serve in leadership roles where people look up to them. Spirit Jezebel is against Godly authority. It opposes truth and God's servants who speak truth. It's cocky and arrogant. Today, spirit Jezebel cannot physically kill God's servants. They kill the character of God's servants with the sword-their tongue. Spirit Jezebel will be dethroned in Jesus' mighty name. Selah †

Just as iron sharpens iron, a person sharpens the character of his friend. REMEMBER, everybody is not a friend. Selah †

Demons hate ministries that confront them and throw them out of God's House (a person's mind, will, emotions and body). That's why you will hear more criticisms on such ministries. Selah †

Sexual demons in God's House. These things should not be. This is why Satan prevent TRUE deliverance ministers from getting invitations to church events. He don't want the pastor and members free from sexual bondage. Selah †

I had to die to self and the LORD done it through criticism of mankind. And it continues. Selah †

It really take humility to receive, especially from someone who have way less than you. Selah †

After I first came to the LORD in 1995, He sent a young girl to me. I ministered salvation to her. She would come over my house and I will talk to her about the things of the LORD. She did this for many weeks. One morning I had to go somewhere with my husband and when we got to the curve of our street, she was standing there. IMMEDIATELY the LORD opened my spiritual eyes and I saw demon spirit fornication. I was shocked and it was shocked because it knew I saw it. When I got home, she IMMEDIATELY came over to the house and started confessing that she allowed her ex-boyfriend to spend the night over her house and they had sexual intercourse and then she left my house. Thereafter, she stopped having any dealings with me. Dear Hearts, you may only had a one-night stand with your ex-boyfriend or girlfriend and repented; but I'm here to tell you that spirit fornication is IN you and you need deliverance in Jesus' mighty name. If not, you will do it again. Selah †

A young man submitted a deliverance request for the first time several years ago. The next year, he submitted another. The next year he submitted another. Then this year, he submitted another. Each time he submitted the request, I will tell him the same thing the LORD told me.

SELAH † THINK ABOUT IT!

That is "His deliverance is in his obedience." Finally, one day he confessed, "Evangelist King, I got angry with you when you told me that my deliverance is in my obedience." I said to him, "I know." Then the LORD brought something to my attention and I began to tell him, "You know, Naaman did the same thing. He got mad with Elisha for not coming out and laying his hands upon him in pronouncing him healed from Leprosy. Instead Elisha just sent his servant to tell him what he should do. Therefore, Naaman's healing and deliverance was in his obedience." Dear Hearts, not all the time we will LIKE what the man or woman of God may do or say. But rest assured, your deliverance is in your obedience to God. Selah †

My daughter shared a dream with me she had. In the dream, I was teaching and preaching and demons looked at me and began to make fun of me. They talked about me. They looked at my clothes and laughed. My daughter noticed that I did not say a word to them, but continued to minister. They looked at my shoes which was torn and laughed. Then SUDDENLY, a thunderous voice said, "TOUCH NOT MY ANOINTED!" They stopped and ran in terror. As she was sharing her dream, the LORD was giving me the interpretation of the torn shoes. I then shouted, HALLELUJAH!!! Dear Hearts, I don't need to defend myself. As long as I DO the will of the Father Who sent me through His Son, Christ Jesus by the Holy Spirit, God will defend His anointed. Selah †

Women, if you have been delivered from demonic bondage, be sure to maintain your deliverance by submitting to God in ALL areas of your life, especially in the area of FAITH or trusting God's Word. Those demons are plotting to come back in and when they do, spirit Jezebel will be the ring leader and then spirit snake. IF they enter, your last state is far worse than your former. So KEEP trusting and believing in God's Word. Selah †

A Believer doesn't practice wrongdoings. He/she may make a mistake; just as King David, they repent and sin no more. But to do wrong continuously, makes one a sinner — someone who practices sin or wrongdoings. Those who DO such things will NOT inherit the Kingdom of Heaven. Selah †

Do you not know that whatever spirit is in a person and they lay their hand upon you that spirit will transfer into you? So make sure you have seen 'fruit of the Holy Spirit' in a person's life BEFORE you walk to that prayer line to have hands laid upon you! NOT ALL HANDS ARE HOLY GHOST FIRE HANDS. Selah †

There are MANY people who have forsaken (or given up) on going to a local church. They browse Facebook every day. Facebook is their church. Therefore, the LORD God places workers on Facebook to speak or post His Word for such people to hear. Making them without excuse when they meet Him face-to-face on that GREAT and TERRIBLE day of the LORD. Selah †

The Holy Spirit is so on point when He gives me posts that a person "thinks" I am talking directly to and about them. Therefore, they take an offense and soon remove me as their Friend. We forget that God's Word is so sharp that it pierce through our soul (mind, will, emotions) and it discern our thoughts. AWESOME! Selah †

Jesus said (paraphrase), when the strongman leaves, it comes back and look to return to his former house, upon finding it just like it likes, it returns. It does not come alone, but bring seven more spirits more powerful than it and the person will be in worse shape than before. Dear Hearts, I have seen this happen too many times. Do you know it's now harder for that person to repent? Selah †

We, God's children, should not be using Facebook to "dump" our emotional garbage. The LORD God told us to dump our cares upon Him because He is the ONLY person who cares for and about us. Selah †

After their deliverance session, I have been told by many that the devil would tell them not to speak to me again. They disobeyed him with the exception of two people and they have refused to verbally speak to me again. Of course, they will make a comment on my posts every now and then, but will not talk directly to me. I'm to the point now that I refuse to "play" with the devil. When the Holy Spirit allow me to see him, I will confront him and that means letting the person know who exactly is in them. Again, I'm not here to make friends with the devil. I'm here to bring Glory to the name of our LORD Jesus. Selah †

A relative once asked, "Why do Terry has to be so different than everybody in the family?" My answer to them is "I was born to be different. My Father (in Heaven) is different. I was born to be just like him through Christ Jesus. Therefore, I act and speak differently and no one can change it. That's who I am." Selah †

KEEP reading my posts, you will learn a "little" about me. Selah †

We cannot take Scriptures and twist it to fit into our own understanding. And whenever someone correct us, we get offended and say offensive things. Out of the abundance of the heart, the mouth speaks or in this case, writes. Selah †

It's not the witches who dress for Halloween we should be concerned about. It's the witches that sit next to us in church services that we should be concerned about. Selah †

Christian witches love Oprah and Iyanla; for they teach "you can do all things without the Anointed One and His anointing". Selah †

Jesus told us, His disciples, that we shall be tested. We shall have MANY trials, but He delivers us out of them all. Now, every time one may experience evil attacks, sickness, pain or etc., does it means that they are not walking in Truth? Of course, not. It may mean that some of the times, but not all of the times. This is why the Apostle Paul told us to work out our own salvation with fear and trembling. We need to search our own heart and the Holy Spirit will let us know whether these things are stemmed from our disobedience or our obedience. In all our getting, let us be sure to get understanding. By doing so, the evil one CANNOT keep us confused and deceived. Selah †

In the beginning of my ministry, even though I did not know much about the LORD God, He supernaturally revealed some biblical lessons to me to write for children of ALL ages. I presented it to my pastor at that time. I was allowed to teach children in age group 8-10. As I was teaching them the lessons, they were very happy and were learning a lot about Jesus. These children have never heard about Jesus because this was a religious organization who only taught about their organization. They NEVER spoke of or about Jesus Christ. At that time, the LORD's grace and mercy led Roger and I to Himself and we were born anew in Christ Jesus. The next day the pastor contacted me and told me not to do that again. He did not care for me teaching the children about Jesus through coloring and drawing. He then notified the headquarters of the church and asked for their advice. Upon reviewing my case, headquarters told him that what I did was perfectly correct. Even though the pastor knew headquarters decision, he refused to allow me to teach the children again and rejected The Children's Mite and taught others to reject it as well. Today, most of those children who were denied to know about Jesus Christ are living a wayward lifestyle. When you reject the LORD's servant, you are rejecting Him. Selah †

It is the carnal mind who says, "I am of Paul. I am of Apollos." Selah †

It had been told about Jesus that he cast out demons by the power of Satan. Therefore, it doesn't surprise me whenever one says the same thing about another man or woman of God. It just shows me the person who is spreading those lies is of their father, the devil. Selah †

People "think" their cigarette smoking only affect them. Have you ever been in a room or car with a chain smoker? The stench of smoke permeates from their entire body and clothes working its way in your air passages. I have been told that second-hand smoke is the worst form of cigarette smoking. I'm here to warn you. Avoid being closed in with a chain smoker. It is detrimental to your health. Selah †

We all have been "hurt" some way or another in the local church. I have MANY testimonies of rejection from the church due to being black or a female and from being black and a female. I have experienced hurts and pains from the church because of being a black female preacher when my husband was accepted because of being a black male preacher. DID I ALLOW THOSE REJECTIONS TO STOP ME? Neither did I give in to Satan's trick in causing me to fall COMPLETELY out with the local church. During those periods of testing, I looked to the LORD God for help and answers in His written Word. He always reminded me that He first was rejected due to various reasons and the same will happen to me. He reminded me that He gave His life for the church and He told me not to give up on assembling with the saints in the local church. Selah †

The greatest joy to a victim of theft is not seeing or hearing that the thieves were identified, but to see or hear that the thieves were identified and arrested. LIKEWISE, whenever one share an audio and/or video clip of how God used them in casting out demons, I don't get joy when seeing and/or hearing demons making themselves known or manifest. I get GREAT JOY when I see and/or hear them leave. Selah †

Believe you receive WHEN you pray—not after you have prayed, but when you pray. NOW, Get Up and thank Him and CONTINUE to thank Him. Selah †

The majority of the time when we do not see any changes in our circumstances, it is because we are battling or fighting against the wrong beings. It is NOT human beings who are causing troubles and/or problems in our life, but demonic beings. Come against them (and not people), in Jesus' name, by submitting to God. Selah †

Many years ago; for His intent and purpose, the LORD God moved my family and I into an area infested with drug users. Late at night, there would be knocks at the door and we were wondering why so many people was coming to our house. After several weeks of living there, the LORD spoke to me and said to make a banner entitled, "Jesus is LORD of this House" and place it over the front door. We then noticed the people stopped coming to our house late at night. We later learned that our house was once the home of a drug dealer. After finding out this information, I praised the LORD God for His protection and said to Him, "LORD, if this is the reason why you allowed us to live in this project housing for this season, send whoever you have chosen for me to help." About a few days later, I heard a knock at the door. I looked and it was my young aunt. I'm only a year older than her. She was a drug user and drunkard. Whenever she gets drunk, she can be VERY worrisome. When I saw it was her, I tried to hide and said to myself, "Dawg! What does she want?" After I said it, the LORD God spoke to me in such a gently way and said, "You told me to send her." I then dropped my head in repentance and opened the door. To this day I am glad I did; because at that very moment, She confessed to killing herself, but she first wanted to talk to me. After our conversation, she stressed how she had changed her mind and was happy to have spoken with me. Dear Hearts, trust in the LORD God with all your heart and lean not to your own understanding. Selah †

Can a person love God, the Father; but dislike His Son, Jesus Christ? The Son says, "No one can come to the Father unless they come first through Me." Therefore, when you reject the Son, you rejected the Father. LIKEWISE, how can one say they love my mother, but dislike me? If you dislike me, you dislike her because I come from her. Therefore, there is no way you can TRULY love my mother without loving me. Selah †

IF you have to live off credit cards in order to live as middle to upper class resident, then you're not middle to upper class. Selah †

Jesus said, "When I am lifted up from the earth, I will draw everyone to myself." Therefore, when we talk about anything other than Jesus Christ, He CANNOT draw the person to Himself. LET'S TALK ABOUT JESUS! Oh, yeah, I forgot. For out of the abundance of the heart, the mouth

SELAH † THINK ABOUT IT!

speaks. Selah †

You know, members in the churches did not LIKE Apostle Paul letters (or posts). They murmured against him and accused him of being bold only through his writings. But the Apostle Paul let them know, in other words, that the same way he is bold through his letters; he is even bolder in their presence. LIKEWISE. Selah †

If I'm an alcoholic and someone buys me a bottle of Hennessy, does that mean it was God who blessed or made me happy? Every time someone or something makes us happy does not mean it was the God who done it. Remember, happiness to the evil one is doing evil in God's eyesight. Therefore, when one leans on their own understanding, it will make them feel happy or blessed; but that feeling is not from God. Selah †

We need to STOP our foolishness. Just because we may "see" the Power of God operating at a certain location and through a certain man or woman does not mean that is the only location or only man or woman the Holy Spirit is operating through. Therefore, why do we only believe unless we go to see such-and-such, then we will not get healed or delivered? Know you not that the Holy Spirit is not limited to one location or through one person. He is doing His MIGHTY work throughout the world in various locations and through various people. Seek the LORD God and not a location or person! Selah †

Whenever demons are involved, counseling will not help! Whatever addiction one may have, counselors cannot TRULY help them. Demons CANNOT be counseled. Firstly, they must be recognized and then by faith in Christ Jesus, His servant COMMANDS them to leave the house (your body). Now, the person is able to remain free as long as they are submitting all their ways to the LORD God. Selah †

So what! When I speak truth, I get attacked. It's STILL not about me, but about Him. It's a privilege and honor to participate in His sufferings, as well as, His blessing. Selah †

The LORD God really hates discord or strife. It causes a person to be against another. Just a tiny drop of discord will cause uproar. IF a person is consistently whispering negative words into your ear against another person, regardless of how much you try not to believe it; you will eventually believe it because of your failure to persistently forbid them in speaking such words. Discord or strife is like poison ivy. When you're in it, it will continue to spread; and the LORD's Presence does not dwell where there is discord or strife. Selah †

As a little girl I loved to sit around my grandmother and hear her share life experiences. She shared with us about a lady preacher in which EVERY time she ministered, she would condemn those who were having babies outside of wedlock. She would preach like this each time. Many years later, someone found her and her daughter dead. Reports revealed that they had committed suicide due to her daughter becoming pregnant outside of wedlock. Dear Hearts, do unto others as you would have them do unto you. Today I watched a video clip that is circulating around Facebook of little girls' "twerking". After watching it, I thought about WHAT IF that was my child. Would I want anyone to share it? No! Instead I would want them to pray for me and my child. The LORD says, "With the same measure we mete, it will be meted back to us." Therefore, with the same measure of mercy we give unto others, it will be given to us. That preacher did not have any mercy or grace toward someone else's child. Therefore, when the same thing happened to her child, she did not have the grace (and her child) to continue in life. Selah †

The one the LORD God has chosen to help you will be the one Satan will cause you to reject. Selah †

Have you noticed that over the years the design of the wedding dress has changed? BEWARE of the mermaid-shaped wedding gown. Selah †

SELAH † THINK ABOUT IT!

He's God when you have your needs (and desires) met. Is He STILL not God when you don't have your needs (and desires) met? We praise Him when he supplies our needs (and desires). Do we STILL praise Him when He doesn't supply our needs (and desires)? Is He worthy (or not) to be praised because He is FAITHFUL. Selah †

How happy is the person who does not follow the advice of the wicked or take the path of sinners or join a group of mockers! Instead, their delight is in the LORD's instruction, and meditates on it day and night. Selah †

A few days ago a young lady became VERY offended at one of my posts. She was so offended she finally believed what her husband had been telling her about me—that I am a "false" prophet. She then removed me from her Friend's list; which was a GREAT favor. She sent a message making it known who she was; and to my surprise, she is sister to another friend of mines on Facebook who the LORD sent to me last year for deliverance. God delivered her and her husband from sexual demons. For MANY months, she would keep in contact with me whenever she needed encouragement in God's Word. I knew by the Spirit of God that Satan wanted her back. Satan tried many times to get her, but he failed. She would constantly stay in contact with me rather through my posts or a telephone call. For the past several days, I felt a nudge to check and see if she was still my Facebook friend. To my surprise, she had removed me. This GREATLY saddens me because I knew that Satan would convince her, through her sister, to have nothing else to do with me so that he can get her back like he want. My heart is SADDENED. All I can do is pray for her. Dear Hearts, we are to love our family; but when family is not walking in the ways of God, we are not to go along with them. The LORD says that whoever loves family or friend more than Him is not worthy to be in His Kingdom. BE CAREFUL! Satan will work against God through family. Selah †

REMEMBER when the LORD God set one FREE, that is ground Satan wants back. Therefore, STAY submitted to God and then you can resist him and he will run from you in terror. STAY submitted to God—not family. Selah †

If you REALLY want to make "trouble" for Satan, START casting out devils! Selah †

Satan doesn't care about you prophesying house, car, land or whatever else material need. As a matter of truth, he will give you those things. He just doesn't want you to THROW him OUT the house—the body. Selah †

The Holy Spirit HELPS our infirmity — our weakness in praying because we don't know what to pray. Selah †

IF you're not pregnant and feel movement in your body, deliverance is needed in Jesus' name. Selah †

Some people say, "Everything bad is not caused by demons and they are not involved." When I hear a person say these words, I wonder if they are on the devil's side. Dear Hearts, evil or bad comes from Satan. EVERYTHING bad or evil stems from him. There is no "nice" way to put it. Selah †

I'm here to tell you that whenever devil(s) are in you, you will have a DISLIKE toward any person speaking (or writing) Truth. Selah †

AFTER the LORD God sets one FREE from demon spirits, don't go and make a joke out of it! You're endangering yourself. Those same demons will house themselves in you! Selah †

Anointing water is just water to us; but to devils, it is poison. Selah †

Some "young" women reject wisdom and Godly instructions and they MUST learn the hard way. During those hard times, some comes out while others don't. Why take that risk? Selah †

SELAH † THINK ABOUT IT!

Have you observed in Scriptures how the angel of the LORD appeared to God's servants? Even though they knew about demons and angels, they mostly spoke about angels. Why is it in today's time, children (of God) speak more on seeing demons than angels? It is NOT proof you're a child of God by "seeing" demons all the time. As a matter of TRUTH, it does not take faith at all to see demons—just obey them and they will make themselves known. On the contrary, it does take faith to see the Kingdom of God. Selah †

A fifth grader does not have the knowledge like a twelfth grader. Therefore, many times the fifth grader will misunderstand the twelfth grader due to lack of understanding. LIKEWISE, some of God's children are more knowledgeable in God's Word than others. Therefore, it will be times whenever they speak or whatever they do; they will be misunderstood. Selah †

Satan has been "twisting" what God has said for centuries. Don't be surprise when the words you have spoken (or written) are twisted. Selah †

IF one offense causes you to DISLIKE a person, that is proof that you did not LIKE the person from the very beginning. LOVE doesn't keep a record of wrongdoings, says the LORD God. Selah †

Many years ago my grandmother's youngest daughter was sick in the hospital. My circumstances did not allow me to go and see her; so by faith, I spoke words of healing in the atmosphere to her. Later that night my grandmother called due to worrying about her daughter. I told her, "Mama. Don't worry. I have already sent the Word. She is healed." The next day her daughter was out of the danger zone. Dear Hearts, what gift we have in this earthen vessel!?! All we NEED to do is BELIEVE HIS WORD. Just believe, do and say. Selah †

Women, some of you may become offended, but it's TRUTH. IF you desire to show off even a little cleavage, there is something in you that needs to come out in Jesus' name. Selah †

When one disobeys the rules, tragedy is a possibility. PLEASE for your sakes (and others) obey traffic rules. OBEY THE SPEED LIMIT. Selah †

The LORD God takes no pleasure in the death of the wicked. He prefers that they turn from their ways and live. Therefore, why do we get pleasure when our enemy suffer and pray they should die? Selah †

A teacher doesn't share ALL knowledge with their student. The student MUST study to further their understanding. Selah †

Many years ago I was in need of help. I needed $500. I'm not the type of person who is proud and refuse to ask for help. I'm just careful about who I ask for help. I knew family and our local church would not help. Now, that's sad to say, but TRUTH. My only friend did not have it and suggested that I ask a certain co-worker. She was a sweet older lady from Germany and our boss who was a Jew treated her badly due to the past. My heart felt I could trust her in that she would keep it a secret and not boast to other co-workers about what she had done for me. I asked her and promised to pay her back on the next pay day. She was willing and VERY happy to help me. The next pay date, I kept my promise to her and paid her back. To this day, she NEVER mentioned to anyone what she had done for me. Dear Hearts, when you TRULY give from your heart, you will not boast about what you have or had done. Selah †

You better THINK before you issue a curse upon someone. You just may be cursing the wrong person. Curses have no power upon a TRUE child of God. Satan also says that his word will not come back to him null and void. Therefore, since your curse will not work on God's child; Satan will redirect the curse upon you, the human sender. Selah †

What's in your heart is what you are drawn to. Have you SERIOUSLY

SELAH † THINK ABOUT IT!

wondered why you're drawn to LIKE people like Criss Angel and David Blaine? I guarantee somewhere in your family lineage there is witchcraft. Deliverance is needed in Jesus' name. Selah †

Do we TRULY believe God will do what He said He would do? Supposedly, you don't have any object that has been anointed by a man or woman of God to use as point of contact for healing and/or deliverance. Will you STILL believe He would do what He said He would do? Selah †

ALL of the miracles, healings and deliverance the LORD God done through the Apostle Paul, he knew it was not him who was doing the works. He also knew he had no power or authority without Jesus Christ. When church members began to speak foolishly about whom they follow, the Apostle Paul sternly corrected them. Let us LEARN from their mistakes. Selah †

CONFESSION is vital. One CANNOT be saved, healed or delivered unless they're WILLING to confess to their wrongdoings (and forsake them). At least Catholics got this one (CONFESSION) right. Selah †

At times your mind is "clueless" in knowing what your spirit knows through the Holy Spirit. Listen to the Holy Spirit and not your mind. Selah †

You say that I am a witch. Supposedly, it was true. Would Jesus Christ want you to mistreat me? No, He wouldn't because His desire would be to save me from my sins so I may live and not die. Selah †

When one is a "true" worshiper of the Father, they will not need a cheerleader to lead them into a pep rally in order to worship Him. Selah †

When a person comes out of the occult and become a Christian, they MUST be extra careful to not tap into the spirit realm on their will. There are MANY pastors who once were spiritualists BEFORE their conversion to Christ Jesus. Some of them, unknowingly and knowingly, are tapping into the spirit realm as they will and are accounting it to the work of the Holy Spirit. I watched a video clip yesterday on YouTube from an international ministry. The pastor/prophet/apostle was commanding people who had sleep problems to sleep. He used the written word to back up what he was doing. When he commanded the people that had problems sleeping to sleep, they suddenly went to sleep. He then showed the people how it was scriptural in commanding people to do certain things. The problem with this is that we are NOT to command people to do anything. We are NOT to control people because they have their own will. Our battle is not with people. It is with spiritual evil beings. The people were told and taught that they have power to control or command people to do whatever they want. Dear Hearts, the spirit of control is witchcraft. Selah †

We need to be "careful". We are to love our family; but when family is willfully practicing evil, this is where we draw a line. We CANNOT go along with their ways when their ways are not in accordance to God's Word. Many family members hate other family members due to someone in the family allowed the Evil One to lie on and about them. Don't fall victim to Satan's trap. IF you have heard something your family member has done or said that will not cause you to love them, you need to inquire about it to that family member who is being talked about. Don't believe the lies that have been circulated. The LORD God once said these words to me, "Terry, there are two kinds of people in hell. 1) Those who spoke lies; and 2) those who believed lies." Selah †

So what! Such-and-such is your enemy and your position and/or circumstances are above them! Does God give you His permission in mistreating them? Repay evil with good. Selah †

Marine demons are sexual demons. Their desire says, "It's all about sex, baby." Deliverance is needed in Jesus' name. Selah †

SELAH † THINK ABOUT IT!

Devils are merciless. Any time we don't show mercy toward others, it is NOT the Holy Spirit who is expressing (or venting) through us. Selah †

It's BAD whenever a runner gets close to the finish line and then drop out of the race. Now, that's sad. REMEMBER, races are not won necessarily by the swift, but by the one who ENDURES TO THE END. WE CAN DO ALL THINGS THROUGH HIS ANOINTING. Selah †

The attitude of Jesus is "Father, forgive them; for they do not know what they're doing." IF Jesus is in us by His Spirit, then it will also be our attitude toward others. Selah †

IF you are one of those who post pictures of yourself on Facebook, then SERIOUSLY ask yourself, "Why am I posting this picture? What message do I want to relay to my friends?" Afterward, discuss it with Jesus Christ to see if He LIKES your reasoning. Selah †

People who don't like TRUTH will ALWAYS say, "It's nobody's business what I do." But the very moment they need help, they cry out to somebody. Whether we realize it or not, what we do or say is Jesus' business and ALL Jesus' business is God's children's business. Selah †

Do you not know that when Jesus walked the earth, He would respond to stiff neck people's comments with holy boldness? There were even times He would get smart with them and STILL continued walking in and with LOVE. Selah †

God only showed Moses His behind parts due to him not being able to live if he saw His face. Therefore, what is the woman's reason in showing her behind parts? Selah †

So you say that the LORD God has blessed you with great finances, a nice car, a wonderful house and etc. Did He bless you just for you to enjoy yourself? Have it occurred to you that He blessed you so that you may bless His orphans, widows and the needy? He has given you more than enough to take care of yourself and others in need. As you give, then you will receive. Help those who CANNOT repay you and the LORD God will repay you for them. BUILD up your heavenly account; and one day, you will be most happy that you did. Selah †

IF I only give to help my own race or family, then I have done nothing because LIKEWISE the wicked. But when I give to help others regardless of their race, gender or religious preference; then TRULY the love of God is in me. For WHOSOEVER will, our LORD God saves, heals and delivers in Jesus' name. Selah †

If you disagree so much with a person, instead of speaking, posting or sharing evil comments about them and getting others to agree with you; go directly to that person and talk about your concern(s). Most times people are really cowards in confronting others so they will post or share comments on social networks voicing their thoughts. This way is contrary to the way Jesus Christ has instructed us. Every now and then I may have someone who disagrees with what I have said and I kindly would ask them to give me a call to talk about it. Instead, they will choose to leave their evil comment and refuse to directly talk with me. Their behavior only proves that they are of their father, the devil who is STILL angry toward Truth, Jesus Christ. We say we are God's children, let us also act like God's child. Selah †

When devil(s) is/are in a person, the devil(s) in the person will despise the person who speaks truth. It's not the person who is doing the despising, but the demon(s) in the person. Just think! A person has not done any wrong toward you and you just don't LIKE them. Who do you think it is who is causing you not to LIKE the person? It's not the Holy Spirit! For the Holy Spirit LIKES ALL people. His desire is to bring EVERYONE to the saving knowledge of Jesus, the Christ. I will never forget the time before I was delivered from demons. For some reason and I could not tell you, I did not LIKE Sarah Bowling, Marilyn Hickey's daughter. I could not tolerate hearing her voice. I immediately claimed that something was wrong with her. Then after my deliverance, and I praise the LORD God for His wonderful mercy and grace, I no longer felt that way about her. Through Facebook, I had the opportunity to share that testimony with her. Of course, it was lengthy and she read it all and responded with gladness. If you find yourself despising or disliking someone, the problem is not in them. It is in you! As with me, deliverance is needed in Jesus' name. Selah †

Just think! Jesus' family members and those he grew up around, the majority of them, rejected him. They talked against him. They spoke and shared lies about him one to another. They hated TRUTH because Jesus only spoke truth due to being TRUTH. Therefore, when that same Jesus, the Christ, is IN you; you too, will be hated and there will be those who will speak and carry lies on and about you from one person to another. Family members who are not in Christ Jesus will reject. So, don't count it as being strange when it happen. It's the norm. Selah †

Respect and obedience are two different meanings. You can respect a person without obeying them and you can obey a person without respecting them. My husband and I not only taught our children to respect their parents, but to obey us in the LORD God and to respect those who are old enough to be their parent. And whenever their elders are wrong, we taught them to respect them, but do not obey their wrong instructions. Dear Hearts, regardless of what a person may do or say, RESPECT them because one day you MUST give an account to your LORD and Master, Christ Jesus, for your actions. I know we have been taught to give respect to where respect is due, but this saying did not originate from God. He instructed us to do unto others as we would have them do unto us. Respect others in Jesus' name. Sometimes it is just BEST not to say a mumbling word and PRAISE HIM. Selah †

As I was giving the website a "new" look, I decided to select the 10 most-viewed deliverance session videos to compile into a carousel. As I was listing them, I thought about each person. On a good note, a few are managing the upkeep of their deliverance; while most of them have lost it.

Dear Hearts, our LORD Jesus Christ is always willing and able to set us free from demonic oppression and depression; but we MUST realize that when He does, we MUST maintain (or keep) our deliverance and that is up to us to do and not Him. Jesus Christ will empower us to do as long as we accept His guidance and leading. He will NOT force us to do anything or to believe Him. We MUST willingly choose to obey Him and walk in His obedience by His Holy Spirit. As I think of the people who are willfully walking in disobedience and have given devils legal rights to ruin their life, it greatly saddens my heart. OBEY HIM AND KEEP HIS COMMANDMENTS. Selah †

Some people closely follow the teaching of men and women who have already left this earth. When they were upon the earth, they refused to follow them. Now since they are gone, they claim the LORD God instructed them to adhere to their teaching and accept no teaching from other living beings. Is this voice TRULY of God? Selah †

We MUST be willing to accept and experience His sufferings as we do His blessings. No one and I mean no one will treat you the way Christ Jesus treats you. Our GREATEST hurt and pain will come through those we love the most, our family. LORD Jesus, have your way in our lives that will bring you glory. Selah †

Many years ago I often visited a family member's house. They would ALWAYS have something bad to say about their child. As I listened to them, I would always agree with them due to the person being VERY close to me. One day as they were talking against their children, the LORD God spoke to me. He said, "Terry, if they speak evil words of their own child, then they are also speaking evil words about you to their child." I thought about it and saw that was truth. From that moment, I stopped listening to them whenever they would speak evil words against their child. I redirected our conversation onto another subject. That person then stopped speaking evil to me about anybody. Dear Hearts, IF your mother, father, sister, brother, aunt, uncle or cousin will speak evil words to you about a family member; then rest assured, they also are speaking evil words about you. Selah †

SELAH † THINK ABOUT IT!

Satan, through beings (rather human or angelic) has been cursing Jesus Christ when he was known as Lucifer in Heaven. He has been doing it for thousands of years and the LORD God has been tolerating it. Satan knows he has a set time for him to be destroyed and his followers. But in the meantime, the LORD God STILL tolerates the abuse to His name. The reason He is tolerating it is because He love human beings and do not want them to be lost in eternal damnation along with Satan and his angels. Therefore, whenever a man or woman of God is being verbally abused and called every name, but a child of God; it is STILL Jesus Christ Who is actually being abused and not the human person. The human person MUST accept Jesus' sufferings and STILL love the human vessels through whom Satan is working through. Therefore, we should NEVER pronounce a curse upon those who abuses us for Christ's sakes. We should pray and love them. AND REMEMBER, we also MUST glory in His sufferings as we do His blessings. Besides, IF Christ Jesus was not in a person, they would not be receiving such abuse from Satan and his team of darkness. Dear Hearts, think about that! Don't get mad whenever you hear Satan through someone curse a man or woman of God. REJOICE for the man or woman of God because they are experiencing His sufferings, as well as, His blessings. And by the way, you MUST do the same when it happen to you. Selah †

I was going through some tough times in my walk with Christ Jesus feeling as though He had left me. One day I came to this realization. I should not question Him but myself. From that day I began to change my prayer to, "Jesus, I know you will never leave me because You said so. Please help me so that I would never leave you." Selah †

Would you accuse Jesus of not speaking in love when He said, "O generation of vipers, how can ye, being evil, speak good things? For out of the abundance of the heart the mouth speaketh." Or when He said, "Go tell that fox (King Herod), 'I will keep on driving out demons and healing people today and tomorrow, and on the third day I will reach my goal." Today, would we accuse Him (and His servants) of not speaking in love? There's a time for ALL things. Selah †

I despise demon spirit Jezebel! I know when it raises it's ugly head. It and spirit snake works together. The LORD my God rebuke you in Jesus' mighty name! Selah †

Women of God! You say you are free and delivered and that is truth. As a child of God, then why would you wear the devil's materials? Know you not that fake hair is the devil's label. Demons have claimed fake hair as their belongings and anyone who wears it; they attach themselves to the person. Does the LORD God truly need to use fake things in order to make us look and/or feel beautiful? He needs nothing fake in order to do that! Therefore, when the LORD God TRULY delivers us, He delivers us from ALL evil. Selah †

Demons know when the LORD God has revealed, to His servant, information about their existence. Therefore, what they do is give thoughts to their host in accusing God's servant that he/she is talking about them. They do this in order to throw LIGHT off themselves and get their host to reject and/or speak evil of God's servant. REMEMBER, this is a SPIRITUAL BATTLE and not a physical one. Selah †

Years ago a person shared their experience with me. They have been smoking for MANY years and continued to smoke cigarettes while serving as a devoted and faithful member of the church. One day, they started experiencing seeing worms coming out of their nose. They went to the doctor and the doctor could not see any proof of them having worms. They kept telling the doctor about the worms they pulled out of their nose and they continued to crawl through their nose. The doctor told them the next time it happened that they should keep it and bring it with them on their next visit. When the worms came from their nose again, they could not grab it. It was then the LORD God revealed to them that the worms were spiritual and caused from their continuing disobedience in smoking cigarettes. The LORD God opened their spiritual eyes to "see" what they TRULY looked like in the spirit realm and they saw worms crawling in and out of their nostrils. Selah †

LEADERSHIP

THE DISCIPLINE OF THE LORD. You may hang around a person; but when certain other people come around, you withdraw due to being ashamed to be with the person. BEWARE of spirit shame! For this the Apostle Paul rebuked Apostle Peter. Selah †

I have observed how some pastors only desire is to raise up a company of pastors under their leadership so they can be looked upon as being a pastor of pastors. This was NEVER Jesus' desire. Jesus' desire was ONLY to DO the will of the Father in Heaven. The Father assigned 12 men (including Judas) to him so he would lead, by his example, them back to the Father. I'm no longer impressed when I see a person having other persons under their direction and leadership. What impress me is to see them DOING the will of the Father and His will is for EVERY man and woman to be TOTALLY free in order to serve Him in spirit and truth. Selah †

Jesus Christ ALWAYS placed emphasis on God's children showing love one to another. It's the second greatest command from Him. IF we don't love, and to put it simpler, LIKE one another; then we will not see the Kingdom of Heaven. For how can we love or like a God whom we cannot see; and hate or dislike our brother or sister who we do see? I'm saddened when I see and know leaders who are jealous of other leaders. They're jealous of how God is using the person. Dear Hearts, that's foolishness. For Jesus Christ said, "Be it according to your OWN faith." We all are working to build the Kingdom of God and not our ministry. Satan is the ONLY person who works to build his kingdom (his ministry) and we're not his children. Therefore, leaders do not need to be in competition with each other. For it is ONLY the Holy Spirit Who give Kingdom increase. Selah †

REMEMBER, leaders are not beyond correction. We don't do EVERYTHING right. Selah †

Do you not know the 5-fold ministry gifts of The Church has nothing to do with rank? They ALL are servants serving servants. Selah †

There are people who don't have access to a Bible, to a preacher, to a pastor or any minister of the Gospel; but yet, The Shepherd, Christ Jesus, reveals Himself to them. Therefore, a sheep without The Shepherd will not reach their destiny. Selah †

Preachers have and are teaching tithes and giving with the wrong motive for a long time. They will stand in judgement for it. And members think their pastor love them so much. Just get in a position where you need their financial help and you'll see just how much they love you. Selah †

Ananias and Sapphira were submissive one to another, but in the wrong way. Look what happened to them! Selah †

I love receiving deliverance requests from church leadership. When the head get right, the body follows. Selah †

I'm not an Evangelist by the will of mankind, but by the will of God. Selah †

Not EVERY speaking invitation is of God! Be careful! Satan only invites his own kind. Selah †

SELAH † THINK ABOUT IT!

My husband and I were invited to hear a person minister at a church. We have never visited the church and didn't even know the pastor. When we got there and took our seat, it was about two hours before the pastor showed up. When she appeared, she was walking like an old lady with a cane. We looked at her and immediately knew she was not of God. Then her co-pastor showed up. I looked at him and immediately saw a fornication spirit. I then looked at the pastor and back at him. I then knew they had a sexual relationship. I didn't say anything to nobody about it. I kept it to myself because the LORD did not tell me to say anything. After the service as we were walking to our car, the person who was invited to speak told us that the pastor called her to the back room and was complaining about us. She said the pastor didn't like us and the pastor then admitted to her that she and her co-pastor had a sexual relationship. Dear Hearts, you'll be surprised to know the number of Christians living together unmarried and hold positions in their local church. These things should not be! Judgment will begin at the House of God! I spoke it long ago in a Holy Ghost FIRE Talk message that pastors (and ministers) are going to drop dead right in the pulpit IF they don't repent and stop their lying ways. Selah †

God doesn't reveal EVERYTHING to His prophets. Some things He will hide from them. Remember, Elisha and the Shunammite woman. Selah †

I'm beginning to clearly see that if you're the type of person that have a problem or think it will become a problem working with the opposite sex in the Kingdom of God; God CANNOT use you. He couldn't use his disciples when he needed the Samaritan woman to be ministered to. So he sent them all away while he calmly went and sat at the well waiting for the woman. He wasn't concerned about how he may look in the eyes of others when talking to a woman. His aim was to carry out His Father's business. LIKEWISE, I'm not concerned (or my husband) whether a person is male or female. This is KINGDOM's business. Selah †

It's becoming a pastoral emergency. Demonic possession on the rise. At least the Catholic priests are trusting God in allowing Him to set captives free through them. What about you, Christian pastors? Selah †

EVANGELIST KING

Yes, when I minister publicly, I wear tennis shoes or flat shoes. It's more comfortable that way. Besides it's not about my looks that matters. It's about the Father's business. Now if you choose to wear your heels, then that's your choice. Don't judge me because I choose otherwise. Selah †

I'm thankful to God that I didn't have to pay monetarily for my training in the Holy Ghost. And I have the BEST Teacher to train me! Hallelujah!!! Selah †

Once a man of God commented on one of my YouTube videos and said that the quality wasn't good. When I read it and looked to see who it came from, I felt discouraged. His comment didn't encourage me at all. I replied and reminded him that it is not the quality of the video that's important. It's the message. He then blocked me from his YouTube Channel. Several years later this same man of God was publicly denied by his mentor and spiritual father. He felt hurt and discouraged. Unknowing to him, I prayed for him because I knew how he felt. Dear Hearts, sometimes we may wonder why certain things happen to us. But think! You just may be a victim of "reaping what you have sown". Selah †

Recently in my ministry, the Holy Spirit is allowing me to see and deal with spirit Jezebel. This spirit is found only in the church among those who claims to be children of God. Just say or do something they feel or think is not of God, you'll know it is there by the person's actions. How defiant it is against any Godly authority; and yeah, it knows Scripture more than you and I. Selah †

MANY years ago my husband and I were members of a church. We were new to the congregation. Now, if you know me, whenever the Word of the LIVING God is spoken, I bear witness by shouting GO AHEAD NOW and AMEN! Well, our pastor invited an Evangelist to minister at the church. He's well-known and is POWERFUL in the Spirit. On the last evening of his visit, I heard God's specific instructions for me. He said, "Terry, I don't want you to sit where you normally sit. I want you to go and stand in the back of the Sanctuary as the man of God minsters and I want you to witness to my Word with shouts of AMEN." I said, "Yes, LORD." So the evening came and I done as the LORD instructed. As I was witnessing to the Word with shouts of AMEN; I observed as the man of God was ministering, a 'religious spirit' in the house. I continued as the LORD instructed until the end of service. On the final morning of our guest, he stood up and said, "I thank God for the young lady who was witnessing to the Word. What she did not know is that she was my strength." That religious spirit in our pastor and the old-schooled members did not and would not open their mouth to witness to God's Word. They were against the man of God and tried to shut him down. PRAISE THE LORD! As Aaron and Hur, God used me to hold up His servant. Therefore; don't let the devil keep your mouth tightly shut! BE A LIVING WITNESS TO THE TESTIMONY OF JESUS CHRIST. Selah †

To be effective, I have learned not to put counseling before deliverance. I'm not here to be a counselor. Often times some people want to be counseled, but they don't want to be delivered from that which is causing them to need counseling. if you desire to be delivered from the 'root' cause of your problem(s), then I'm here to help you. Then, you'll be FREE to receive counseling. Selah †

As time goes on, people are becoming more and more demonized. Demons are getting so bold in making themselves known due to not being threatened. I'm seeing more video clips of demonized people in various places. The saddest part is those who capture these appearances doesn't even know the person is demonized. They think it's funny and share it on Facebook and/or YouTube for views hoping it goes viral. You know, I'm TRULY seeing that Satan doesn't tear his own kingdom down. Demons know exactly who to not manifest in the presence of and that's a TRUE child of God who is walking and using their authority in Christ Jesus. Selah †

Living in the USA where there are different nationalities and culture, as a minister of the Gospel, we shouldn't be satisfied in our heart just ministering to our own race or culture. We should be storming Heaven with our request to minister to all nations who are living within the USA.

When we think of nations, we usually think of other countries. We don't realize in America, we have people from every nation. Therefore, we should be, as ministers of the Gospel, be ministering to ALL people who consist of ALL nations within the USA. The point is don't become satisfied in just ministering the Gospel of Christ Jesus to ONLY your nationality or culture. Constantly remind God of His promise that He has given us the nations; and then, make yourself friendly in order to have friends. Selah †

When going to India-a place where over a billion false gods reside-to minister deliverance and healing, it's BEST to have intercessors 24/7 interceding for you and your ministry team. Now, if you're just going there to talk and take no action, then no worry. Their gods won't even try to harm you. Selah †

When Roger first became aware of his ministry gift from the LORD-the Office of Prophet-he pursued it with all his heart. To gain more understanding, he attended classes, workshops, conferences, seminars and etc. He often visited churches where pastors flowed in that direction. The reason I say all of that is just because my husband was chosen and placed in that office gift doesn't mean I have been chosen and placed in that office gift, too. We would visit people and they would automatically 'think' that I was a prophet along with my husband. When they saw that I did not give them 'a word', they looked down on me. Dear Hearts, just because the husband (or wife) may be called to be a pastor, prophet, apostle, evangelist or teacher doesn't necessarily mean that his wife (or husband) is called in an office gift. I know it 'looks' good for both husband and wife to be in the five-fold ministry; but looks don't have anything to do with it. The five-fold ministry gifts are distributed as the Holy Spirit wills and not as a husband or wife wills. Selah †

It is one thing for a church member to be a gossiper; but when it's a pastor, WOE!!!! Selah †

Was Jesus being compassionate when he said to a man in Luke 9:59-60 (CJB): To another he said, "Follow me!" but the man replied, "Sir, first let me go away and bury my father." Yeshua said, "Let the dead bury their own dead; you, go and proclaim the Kingdom of God!" LIKEWISE, they will say His disciples are not compassionate. Selah †

The purpose of Evangelists and Pastors is not competition. One should not usurp the other authority. They are to work together. In fact, they need each other. The responsibility of the Evangelist is to "PROCLAIM" the Goodness of God with Power and Authority of the Holy Ghost in order to destroy the works of the devil in setting captives FREE. Once they are free, it is when the Evangelist need the Pastor (and the Pastor need the Evangelist). The person then need to be nurtured and feed the Word of God the remaining of their days upon this earth so they can grow into a mature child of God not needing the milk of the Word all the time. This is the reason churches are not growing. They may grow in physical numbers, but not in spiritual numbers. The five-fold ministry gifts of the Church is needed—ALL are needed—and these gifts will not be distributed to just one individual in the local church—the Pastor. They are given or distributed as the Holy Spirit chooses. After the LORD God send His dear children to me for deliverance from demonic oppression that don't have a local church home, my heart grieves because I know they TRULY need a pastor to lead and teach them in TRUTH. It saddens me because the majority of pastors that I do know, I cannot recommend them because they 'think' I am their competition or they are not walking in or teaching truth. TRULY, as the LORD says, the harvest is GREAT, but the laborers are few. Dear Hearts, let us pray with ALL our heart for the leaders of the church. Selah †

Don't become happy just because people seem to accept you. As Jesus upon this earth, when you continue to speak and do truth, they will one-by-one walk away from you. Rejoice for your reward is GREAT in Heaven (and on earth). Selah †

I recently had to move my office from downstairs to upstairs due to family changes. A few weeks later I noticed there was not much privacy in doing deliverance sessions. I would still do sessions, but I began to notice I was not doing as many. Some days I would not do any at all due to non-privacy. After a few months our family situation changed and it gave me an opportunity to move my office back downstairs. My daughter thought about the situation and said, "Momma, even though you're not doing deliverance sessions like you use to, you are still a threat to the devil." When she said these words, the LORD immediately said to her, "A non-active threat is not a threat." Dear Hearts, it's in the DOING that threatens the devil. Selah †

A minister of God CANNOT be withdrawn and feel strange when meeting new people. In the Household of faith, we're not strangers to one another. We're family—the family of God. Therefore, when I meet you, we're family and not strangers. Selah †

Not EVERY ministry opportunity or invitation that comes from India (or any other part of the world) on Facebook is of God. You just may be promoting a pastor who beats his wife and his wife leaves for another man. Selah †

Some deliverance ministers get pleasure out of 'stirring' demons up in a person. My aim is not to merely stir them up; but to cast them out. For this gives me GREAT pleasure when they are up and out in Jesus' mighty name. Selah †

Remember, Jesus had over 500 disciples following (and liking) him. But as He spoke and done things, one-by-one they got offended and disliked him and walked away. Jesus then looked at the 12 and said, will you leave too. Selah †

There are MANY prophetesses and apostles who are carrying in their bellies spirit Jezebel and snakes and folks are allowing them to lay their hands upon their head. You wonder why you have such headaches and body aches. We're living in a generation of vipers, under cover in God's house. Don't be fooled by their good-sounding preaching and teaching. I pray as the LORD opened the spiritual eyes of a young man to TRULY see the demon that was coming at night raping him, I pray the LORD will open your spiritual eyes to see these teaching demons in such prophetesses and apostles. Selah †

REMEMBER, there are demons who are good preachers and teachers. So stop judging a person as being a man or woman of God when they preach or speak well. It's by their 'fruit' you shall know them. Oh, what a gullible generation says the LORD! Selah †

As the Apostle Paul let us know, he had a thorn in the flesh. You know, a thorn in the flesh is a nuisance. If not removed, it continues to buffer or poke at you. There was something that not all the time, but sometimes irritated the Apostle Paul and he wanted Christ Jesus to stop it by removing it. Jesus Christ would not and reminded Paul of His mercy and grace was all he needed. Dear Hearts, we as God's child as the Apostle Paul has a thorn that irritates our flesh. As for me, it seems like I been dealing with this same issue over and over again. Now, I realize today that it is my thorn in the flesh. You know, since coming to the LORD God and being a woman of God; and it only happens in the church, the men (most of the time the male leaders) when they want to know more about me, what I do or want me to know what I should not be doing; they don't come directly to me, but go to my husband and ask or tell him what they want me to know. 100% of the time the things they tell him to tell me does not build love in his heart toward me. They act as though I do not have a mouth to talk; but think since coming to my husband and not me, they have done it the Biblical way. Once I was worshiping in church service and I was doing it quietly. I was in the Presence of God. So we went home and then I heard the LORD say, "Terry, the pastor didn't like it when you were standing up worshiping me. He's going to have his elder call Roger and tell him to tell you." I said, "Yes, LORD." Then I told Roger what the LORD had just said to me. Dear Hearts, it wasn't even two minutes after I told Roger that the phone rang. He answered and it was one of the elders of the church and he told Roger exactly as the LORD told me. We never attended that church again. Over the years, more things happened pertaining to this subject and even till now. Just as the LORD God told the Apostle Paul that his mercy and grace is sufficient; LIKEWISE, I look to his mercy and grace to keep this thorn in the flesh under control. People don't realize it, but women in God and working in the ministry goes through a more intense battle than men all because of people's misunderstanding of God's Word concerning women keeping silent in the church. Therefore; dear hearts, don't do as some. IF you want to know what I do and want me to know what I shouldn't be doing; don't go to my husband and tell him so he can tell me. Come directly to me. For this is the correct biblical way. Selah †

Pastors, not every idea, salvation, healing, deliverance or miracle God will be using your wife to do it. He uses whomever He chooses. Selah †

A pastor was called to the house of a man in his church. He and his elder went. When he got there, he saw that the man's wife was demonized. He commanded the demon to come out of the woman in Jesus' name. The demon then looked at his elder and said, "He's why I am here." The demon came out and the elder later confessed to sleeping with the woman. Dear Hearts, be AWARE when casting out demons. Make sure your own life is aligning with God's Word. Demons will tell on you! Selah †

Is it not foolish for an employee that works in the Financial Department to refuse to have anything to do with any employee who works in the IT Department or Customer Service Department? It's foolish because they all work for the SAME employer; but in different ministrations. LIKEWISE, the Kingdom of God. Selah †

My "heart" goes out to true pastors—shepherding a "mixed" flock. I pray for you wholeheartedly. Selah †

Many ministers of the Gospel complain about people using their name and/or ministry to fraud people into giving them their money. Don't complain too much. REMEMBER, Jesus Christ has been tolerating MANY in using His name to fraud people for thousands of years. Selah †

Jesus, the Christ, shares everything that belong to Him with us — with

SELAH † THINK ABOUT IT!

one exception — His Glory. He will not or ever share His Glory. All glory and honor belongs to Him. Therefore, regardless of how much His anointing is poured upon you; whenever Satan, through people, start to exalt you as though the Power of God belongs to you, you QUICKLY forbid them in praising and honoring you and turn the spotlight onto Jesus Christ. You better do this if you desire to continue living on this earth. Selah †

Why do you think Jesus waited for the Samaritan woman to come at the well? The main reason is that our LORD knew that women can be VERY persuasive. The Father had a plan for this woman. She had spent her life persuading men in the wrong direction. He wanted to use her in persuading men in the right direction; but before He could do that, He had to give her a change of heart. Apparently this woman was so persuasive, she convinced not some, but ALL the men in the city to come and meet Jesus, the Christ. Therefore, men (of God), make sure when you give ear to a woman, she is giving ear to Jesus. Selah †

There was a woman who became offended at what I said to her. She stressed her complaint to several prophetesses. They then concluded that I was a witch. The lady then made nasty comments on our Facebook page and referred to me as a witch. She then continued to spread the word that I was a witch to her friends on Facebook. As I ALWAYS say to people, it is their choice in receiving truth. I refuse to argue. I knew this lady would not have peace in her heart due to rejecting the Word of God because she was not rejecting me. I knew before she could receive peace from God, she had to apologize. I waited and about a year later, she PRIVATELY sent a Facebook message asking forgiveness. Dear Hearts, whenever someone wrong you, it's just a manner of time they will see LIGHT. Forgive them in advance. For our LORD had forgiven us. Selah †

Devils are angry whenever you throw them OUT of the house in Jesus' name! Selah.

SINCE seeing TRUTH, my heart has compassion for ministers who are well-known. They are surrounded with MANY friends; but often, they are alone. MANY claim to love them; when in TRUTH, they only love them due to what they "think" they can GET from or out of them. TRUE LOVE does not seek to GET, but to GIVE. Selah †

Whenever pastors fall from God, the blame cannot be placed on their members due to their lack of prayer. Each man (or woman) MUST give an account to God based on what they have done (not what others have or not have done for them). Selah †

Many years ago there was a sister who became friends with my husband and me— thinking we were part of the in-crowd at church. Upon finding that we were not, she stopped fellowshipping with us. She knew God used us mightily, but choose to be part of the in-crowd instead. After many months in not seeing her, my husband and I heard a knock at the door. We opened the door and it was her. When we looked at her, we noticed a spirit of heaviness upon her. She humbly asked us to pray for her because several weeks ago she had someone lay hands on her to pray; and when they finished, she experienced heavy attacks in her life. Without hesitation, we commanded that dark spirit out of her in Jesus' name. Dear Hearts, there will ALWAYS be those who will refuse or reject you for some "strange" reason; but rest assured, whenever they truly need help, they know who to go to. Selah †

I have encountered quite a few men who say they have no problem with a female minister, but their reactions dictates otherwise. All I need to do is just start talking while in their presence and an uneasiness surfaces. Selah †

Years ago my husband met a native African pastor when we were living in Maryland. He knows I love the company of native Africans. He told me about him and his ministry and I was VERY excited to attend their church service. We went. After the service, he invited us to stay over for the church fellowship dinner. I was so excited to attend after church service. He gave my husband and me a seat next to him. I was so excited and wanted to hear all about them and their ministry. He began to share his story. I then started sharing mines. As I was sharing my story on the LORD's vision through me, I noticed he was getting uneasy. I wondered to myself what his problem was. I continued to talk and he got worse. He then looked over at my husband who was sitting next to me. I then realized that he had a serious problem and I stopped talking. He got up and went away. I then knew, by the Holy Spirit, that he had a problem with authority; and especially a woman who speaks with authority in Christ Jesus. Many months later we moved back to North Carolina. My husband and I found him on Facebook and we became Friends. I noticed that as a minister (pastor) of the Gospel, his posts were not scriptural. I didn't say anything about it. One day he shared a video clip about Prophet Kenneth Hagin, Sr. We happened to have the full video of that service. The creator of the video clip manipulated the video to meet his opinion of Prophet Hagin and the service. I was shocked to see that a pastor of the Gospel went along with this person's opinions. I then "kindly" told him that we should not believe EVERY video that someone makes. I shared with him how easy it is to be deceived. I even told him that we have the full service of the video and the video clip is incorrect. Well, he did not like what I said and removed me from his friend's list. I told my husband about it and he then saw he had removed him, too. AGAIN, there are MANY men who SAY they do not have a problem with a female minister; but I am here to say, their reaction dictates otherwise. ALSO this pastor eventually left his parent church due to not accepting authority. Selah †

If your profession is insurance, you sale insurance. If your profession is photography, you take pictures. Whatever your boss chosen for you to do, you do it. Therefore, my Boss has chosen me to promote love, care and concern. My profession is ministering salvation, healing, deliverance and giving in Jesus' name. Selah †

Leaders supposed to set "good" examples for others to follow. IF a leader doesn't obey rules, then they should not expect their followers to obey their rules. One of Facebook's policies or rules is that we should not create multiple accounts. If they find out that one has broken this policy or rule, then without notification all their accounts will be terminated. Dear Hearts, we as children of the Most High God, let us obey this rule; for

Jesus said to render to Caesar what is Caesar and to the LORD what is the LORD. Selah †

When needing help in the local assembly, at least the Apostles choose men "FULL of FAITH and the HOLY SPIRIT" and not men "FULL of lust, greed and pride". Selah †

If a man will not allow the LORD God to use him in proclaiming His Word, He will use a willing and obedient woman. Don't become jealous when He does! Selah †

My spirit is drawn to TRUTH, Jesus Christ. When I "hear" TRUTH, my spirit LEAPS and SHOUTS for joy. Many times in church service as the pastor would speak TRUTH, my spirit would SHOUT LOUDLY in adoration and praise to the King of kings. Most pastors compared my shouting to me being their cheerleader. I would then look to the LORD in my spirit and say, "Jesus, they don't know. I'm not their cheerleader, but yours." Then when they fail to speak TRUTH, I get quiet. I actually had members to say to me that whenever they needed to know rather the pastor was speaking truth or not, they would just look at me. Dear Hearts, TRUTH is LIFE and gives LIFE. Without Him (TRUTH), we CANNOT survive. LOOK to TRUTH, Jesus Christ, for ALL your needs. Selah †

REMEMER, Jesus had more than 500 men or disciples following Him. As He continue to do and speak TRUTH; due to their lack of understanding, they became offended of His words and the things He done. They one-by-one abandoned or left Him. LIKEWISE, there will be those who may start out LIKING you; but as they continue to follow you, due to their lack of understanding, they will become offended at your words and have nothing else to do with you. REMEMBER, our LORD Jesus STILL ask, "Is the servant greater than their master?" Selah †

The master is greater than the servant. Therefore, my heart's desire is to be MORE in close and personal relationship with the Master rather than

SELAH † THINK ABOUT IT!

the master. Selah †

To men who don't believe that the LORD God uses women: In the beginning of my walk with the LORD, He commissioned me to spread His Good News. When He instructs one to do something, they MUST do it. There's no way around it. Satan voiced his concern to me through men just like you. He tried EVERYTHING to get me to be quiet and not speak or talk about the Holy Name—Jesus. In the beginning, he almost shut me up; but as I continued to keep my focus on the LORD God, I continued to do and speak the things pleasing to Him. Today is a different situation and I'm not that weakling as I was in the beginning. By overcoming Satan's onslaughts through men like you, I am immune to his attack in this area. You can believe and say whatever you want about "the woman preacher". As long as the Good LORD give me breathe in my lungs, I will PROCLAIM with a LOUD VOICE, JESUS IS LORD to the glory of God, the Father. Selah †

A Word of Advice to Deliverance Ministers: The word "your" is possessive. Anything possessive belongs to the person. Whenever you know a person have demons IN them, NEVER speak to the person as if they have ownership of the demons by saying "your demons". Demons DO NOT belong to us. They are thieves and intruders. It's LIKE whenever someone places an object in your home and someone else finds it and say this is your object and then you will say to them, it doesn't belong to me. Throw it out! Therefore, we should not refer to demons in a person as their demons. Selah †

Let's be SURE that we're INDEED free from demons within before we become adamant that we are FREE; for stubbornness goes two ways—right and wrong. Selah †

Since I'm not a "whooping" preacher, most Black churches do not like the way I minister. My aim is not to assist you in "feeling" good. It is to deliver a simple message so that you can understand EVERY word that comes out of my mouth in Jesus' name so you can be FREE. Selah †

EVANGELIST KING

Due to a person's excitement after listening to a "whooping" preacher, I have asked them, "What was the message?" Their response, "I don't know, but he sure can preach." Selah †

I was raised in church listening to a "whooping" pastor; and not only did he whoop, but he also sung as he whooped. I TRULY thought that was the way a person should sound preaching. He would also do the same when he prayed. I noticed EVERYBODY in church did it. One day the pastor asked for everybody to pray, including the young people. I thought to myself, "I can't sing like that!" A Voice then said to me, "Terry, just pray the way you know how to pray." So I prayed in a normal tone without whooping and singing. Of course, the people and the pastor did not like it. He never asked everybody to pray again. Then when I became an adult and TRULY gave my life to the LORD, he commanded me to preach His Word. I then said to Him, "I cannot whoop and/or sing sermons." He then said, "Terry, be yourself. I work with your personality. You don't need to be like the way people think you should be. Open your mouth and I will speak through you." Dear Hearts, And He does! He speaks through me as I open my mouth in faith. You don't need to be like anyone. The LORD God did not make you a clone to anyone. You are an original. Be yourself in Jesus' name. Selah †

The disciples stopped a group who were imitating Jesus in casting out devils and healing the sick due to not being a part of their group. They thought they did a good thing for Jesus in stopping them. When they mentioned it to Him, Jesus rebuked them by saying not to stop them. Dear Hearts, just because a person is not part of your group does not mean they are not doing the will of God. And when a person is not part of your group, REJOICE that the same Jesus Christ Who is acting through your group is also acting through their group. REMEMBER, a kingdom divided will fall; and those who are for Jesus Christ is not against Him and are gathering with Him.   Selah †

The reason why some leaders does not teach or instruct young women in doing right in reference to their body is because they are hoping to get with them, too. Selah †

SELAH † THINK ABOUT IT!

Sadly, the demon spirit Jezebel is working through many women who are calling themselves a prophetess. Since encountering that demon spirit on several occasions in deliverance sessions, the LORD God has allowed me to know when it is speaking and acting, especially through women. The main way to know when this demon spirit is operating in and through a woman is when she is adamantly against any type of authority, especially Godly authority. And what a foul mouth it has! I don't tolerate such spirit. I will love the human person; while at the same time; rebuke the demon spirit in Jesus' name.   Selah †

Why is it that we will respect someone who we consider to be a GREAT man or woman of God; but when it comes to someone who we do not consider to be a GREAT man or woman of God, we will quickly disrespect them? Who is it that we are TRULY serving? Is it mankind or God? IF we are TRULY serving the LORD Jesus Christ, we will respect ALL men or women of God and they will be GREAT in our eyesight as they are in His sight. Selah †

Judas chose to commit suicide as his way-out. He had the same opportunity as the other disciples and could have chosen life, but he didn't. Jesus also was tempted by Satan to commit suicide when he was in the wilderness, but he chose not to do it and to LIVE by EVERY Word that came out of His Father's mouth. We, too, have that same opportunity. Therefore, choose LIFE and live to give God glory on earth as it is in Heaven. Selah †

Jesus allowed His enemies to bound, beat and mock him because it was His Father's will. Jesus did not "think" of himself. He only thought of the Father's plan for his life. The Father loved His enemies so much that He gave His only loving and unique son to be bound, beaten and mocked so that through Him, we may return to His presence. Therefore, when He looks on us, He sees His Loving Son, Jesus Christ. Dear Hearts, thank Him for your enemies! For He died for them, too. Selah †

I'm sure some Catholics don't agree with what some Christians are doing and vice versa. There's one thing that some Catholics does that some Christians does and that is casting out demons. Demons only come out in the Name of Jesus. So why are some Catholics against Christians and some Christians against Catholics? Let's just agree on the TRUTH that each group confesses. IF a Catholic priest is driving out demons and a Christian is driving out demons, then leave them alone. All that matters is that our LORD Jesus Christ is acting through the person in getting His house cleaned and in order.   Selah †

I once dreamed that I was warning a man about not going a certain way due to danger that was detrimental and will cause death. I knew the danger was there because I had seen it. In spite of warning him, he chose to continue traveling in that direction. I cannot describe the feeling I had as I was seeing him go in that direction in spite of the warning. I had such love and compassion for him and then I woke up. As I thought on the dream, my heart was saddened. It is so sad whenever a person refuse to heed to TRUTH through you only because you are a female and/or you are their wife, mother, sister, aunt or cousin.   Selah †

Dear Hearts, whatever we have been chosen to DO for the LORD God, it may "look" like we are the only one doing it; but we are not. IF you are a deliverance minister or ministry, your ministry is NOT the only ministry the LORD God is using to cast out demons. Your ministry is NOT number one or the top ministry. Elijah made that same comment and was rebuked. The LORD God has so MANY ministers and ministries who are unknown in public media who are casting demons out of people. True, there is ONLY ONE and His name is Christ Jesus. Besides He is THE ONE and THE TOP. The rest of us are only following in His footsteps. PRAISE HIM instead of yourself.   Selah †

We had, from elementary to university level, good and bad teachers. The same is true for the Church. There are many teachers, but not all are chosen by the Holy Spirit and placed in that Office Gift. When one has not been chosen by the Holy Spirit and placed in that Office, the end result will be confusion of mind to the student. Selah †

SELAH † THINK ABOUT IT!

Once I was told by a prophetess, "I can't read you." I smiled because I knew she was trying to read me like she was reading others. So in the spirit realm, I took my authority in Christ and forbid it. Dear Hearts, the Holy Spirit doesn't have to 'read' us because He 'knows' us. Selah †

As Jonah; in certain situations, some TRUE prophets will get angry when a person repent. Thank God for His grace and mercy and for not being as mankind. Selah †

PARENTHOOD

If you have teenage children who are sexual active living with and around your children, be watchful! One sexual demon opens the door to other sexual demons and molestation, incest and perverseness are a few of them. The teenage child CANNOT stop themselves from doing such things because of being possessed and/or oppressed by demons within. They may repent of their wrongdoings, but they're not TOTALLY free within and they will find themselves doing the same thing again. This is the VERY reason why deliverance is needed in Jesus' mighty name. Do as the mothers and/or fathers in Scripture. Take yourself and your child to the man or woman of God and ask to be FREE in Jesus' mighty name. Selah †

When I was a teenager, my step-father would often say to my mother. Be careful where you let that girl spend the night. I couldn't understand why he would say those words. Being the only child, often I would get bored so I spent the night with relatives and friends. In my later years, I finally saw truth as why my step-father said that. Dear Hearts, be careful where you allow your child to spend the night. Your relatives or friends may be, unknowing to you, into witchcraft and your child just may see and hear dead people. Selah †

We often see our children doing the opposite of whatever we tell them to do. When they do it, they 'think' they are hurting the parent; when in TRUTH, they're hurting themselves. LIKEWISE, some children of God will do the opposite of what God says through His servant. Thinking they are rejecting God's servant; when in TRUTH, they are rejecting God. It just shows that some child-like behaviors don't need to be carried over into

SELAH † THINK ABOUT IT!

adulthood. Selah †

The BEST way for us (mothers) to teach our daughters (Proverbs 31) is by our example. Selah †

I remember the wayward lifestyle my mother displayed to me from the age of five up to her new life in Christ Jesus when I was around twelve. After her conversion, I greatly respected her because she NEVER tried to conceal her wrongdoings and act as though she never did anything wrong. As a matter of truth, she would always remind me of the wrong she had done and would credit the LORD God whenever I would do the opposite of what she had done. If she was wrong, she would quickly apologize to me; even after the pastor made mention in one of his sermons that a parent should never apologize to their child. I observed her new life in Christ Jesus; and by her example, she taught me the Proverbs 31 woman. Selah †

We do not need to mutilate the organs in our body in order to get the results we desire. After the birth of our third daughter, I decided not to have any more children. Instead of trusting the LORD God in our matter, I decided to help God out by having my tubes tied. I was told that the chances of having children would be one out of a million. After a little over a year, I happened to be that one. On our way to work, I became seriously sick with pain. I told my husband to take me to the hospital. Upon arriving, the emergency room was packed. I had to wait. I was so sick I could not sit or stand. I thought I was lying on my husband's lap, but later my husband told me that I had lain on the floor. As the nurses watched me, they saw that my case was serious and called me ahead of everyone. I was unaware of my surroundings. The doctor took tests and came back with his findings. He said, "Well, Ms. King. It looks like you're pregnant." I could just barely speak. Now thinking about it, the Good LORD allowed me to be aware of things so that I could whisper these words, "Pregnant. I can't be. I had my tubes tied." When the doctor heard those words, he immediately ordered another test. The test revealed that the pregnancy was in the tubes and had burst. Dear Hearts, I was only minutes away from death. They quickly rushed me to surgery. Days after surgery, I walked to the Pediatrics Section of the hospital to look at the babies. I was so used to seeing a baby after my pregnancy; but this time, my heart grieved because there was no baby. It was then that I realized what I had done was not pleasing in God's eyesight. I was sorry in my heart for what I had chosen to do and I thanked the LORD God for His mercy and grace in not allowing me to die. I then knew that my baby was with Him. Roger even said that the LORD told him the gender of our child. It was a boy. We do not need to mutilate the organs in our body in order to get the results we desire. Just trust God and whatever happens; REMEMBER, it will result in no sorrow. Selah †

I wrote many posts on parents buying their children demonic video games to play. A woman replied to one of those posts and said after she saw my post, she became so angry that she went out and bought as many games as she wanted. She thought she was hurting me; when in truth, I was not aware of her doings. A few months later, she cried out to me for help. Sadly, there are just as many parents playing zombie games than children. Selah †

Some people think it's funny (and cute) whenever little girls shake their booty. But when those same little girls become pregnant at 12 or 13 years of age, they don't think it's so cute. Selah †

Some parents are misjudged based on what their child does. They are told, "Train up a child in the way he should go: and when he is old, he will not depart from it"; but do their judges TRULY KNOW what that means. Don't forget! That child has their own will and as they become older, they choose which direction they want to go. Parents should ALWAYS train their children in the way of the LORD; then as they grow older, they will not forget TRUTH. But it does not mean they will choose to continue going in that direction. It means they will not forget it. They are aware of TRUTH and need to make a decision. A decision can only be made when there are at least two choices. They make their choice as to good or evil; life or death. Therefore, STOP misjudging parents based on what their grown children are doing. Instead PRAY. Besides we, as God's children, know TRUTH and some of us are choosing to disobey Him. Does that mean our

SELAH † THINK ABOUT IT!

Heavenly Father is a terrible Father? No! It's our choice as to which way we choose to continue to go because He has given us our own free will. Selah †

It's not often that we visit people homes; but whenever the LORD says to me, "I need you to go to their house", I have learned that it is for a specific reason. The reason would always be for a "spiritual housecleaning". A local couple came to us several months ago for deliverance from spirit spouses and the spirit of lust. The LORD God ministered healing and deliverance and the strongholds were dispelled. After the husband's deliverance, he would often fall back into the temptation of lust and would chat with girls on his mobile phone and a female spirit would attack him at night while he slept. As I heard about these attacks, the LORD instructed me not to say anything to him about it. They decided to visit House Shalom Church service for June. It was at this service when the LORD quietly said to me as I was operating the camera, "I need you to go to their house." After the service, I calmly walked to the wife and said, "It's time. I need to go to your house." She IMMEDIATELY replied in joy, "PLEASE. Come." We made arrangements and last evening we took the one hour trip to their home. When we arrived, we saw they had such a beautiful and huge house. It was well-decorated with many objects. Immediately my spirit geared to the room on the right. I then noticed other objects. I told the LORD that He would have to open a way for us to speak to them about some objects. We then talked for a long while and ate. As we were at the end of our dinner, my husband suddenly asked the wife, "How many clocks do you have in your living room?" She began to count them. He then pointed out other clocks that were in other rooms. Her husband pointed out other clocks in which we did not see. My husband then asked her to come with him to her dining area, in which she had many angels, beautiful decorated urns and chalices. The LORD revealed to our second daughter about the huge mirrors she had in her living room. She told the wife about one of the mirrors, "The mirror consisted of three circles intertwined, much like the Celtic designs in pagan religions. Snake motifs are often found in Celtic designs; however, within everyday household furniture and décor, they are abstracted so that at first glance they won't appear to be so. In this particular mirror, the snakes were disguised as "foliage" embroidered around the outsides of the mirror, intertwining and appearing much like snakes." Our third daughter shared with her the vision she had when we were on our way. She said that the LORD showed her house to her and she saw a black figure walking up the stairs. As my daughter was telling her, I then looked at one of the angels in which she had about three of them. It was a female angel in a green long dress that flowed with the wind. I then said to them, "I would not be surprised if you or your family has seen this demon spirit. This is the female demon spirit that is attacking you at night." There were also MANY videos that consisted of magic and witchcraft that the father had bought for his son's enjoyment. As we pointed out these objects, we allowed them to make a decision in what they wanted to do. The LORD God only wanted us to point these things out to them. I then suggested about three times to the wife how she could go to a Christian bookstore and purchase objects that would lead a person to Jesus Christ as they looked on it. After the third time of mentioning it, she finally said, "I know. I have those things in my shed outside. I don't know what happened to me to take them down and replace them with these objects. The LORD has been warning me about these things through other people and I just ignored them. I'm tired now and want to receive EVERYTHING the LORD has for me. My husband and I will pack all of these things up and destroy them. I thank the LORD for you and your family in helping us to see truth." Dear Hearts, God is so good. He does not want ANYTHING to come between us and Him. He cleans His house (us) and we need to clean our house (our physical dwelling place). Stay blessed in Jesus' name. Selah †

Parents "think" whenever they allow their children to watch cartoons or play video games, it help them in causing the child to become quiet. What a subtle trap from the enemy! In TRUTH, most cartoons and video games are demonic and FULL of witchcraft. Parents may "think" their child or children are quiet; but in truth, they are "quietly" receiving demonic spirits into their mind, will, emotions and body; and in some cases, their spirit. As the child gets older, the "quiet thing" in them manifests into rebellion, anger, hate, rage, murder and promiscuity. Selah †

Parents "think" whenever their child or children plays mom and dad games it is harmless. It's not! That game was not a game suggested by the Holy Spirit for a child to play. It was suggested by the evil ones. Whenever a child or children play "mom and dad", the demon spirit of lust will enter them; and they will eventually start to masturbate, watch pornography and demon spirits of incubus and succubus will enter them causing them to lie on top of each other. This was the "root" way in which a 24 year old girl was demonized and started masturbating at the age of 10. BEWARE! Watch the games your children play. Selah †

RELATIONSHIPS

When I was a young child there was a woman who had an affair with a married man. That's something I have ALWAYS been against because I feared the LORD God. God hears the cries of children and He will repay the adulteress and adulterer. My grandmother often talked about the woman bragging about stealing the woman's husband. The man's wife was a humble woman and refused to retaliate. Many years later when I was in my late teens, I visited her house because I was friends with her daughter. Her daughter took me in the bedroom and it was then I saw the woman. She was bedridden and suffering with some type of illness. I immediately thought about how she had treated that woman in stealing her husband. That same man was still there. Dear Hearts, you will reap what you have sown. When you steal another man's wife or a woman's husband, and it doesn't matter if you marry him or her, you are committing adultery and will suffer for it. Just because the church is doing it doesn't make it right. MANY church people will be very surprised when they see Jesus and He say, "Depart from me, you adulterer or adulteress." Selah †

When your spouse have an affair on you the first thing that comes to mind is to repay them back by having an affair. But if you are in love with Jesus, you will not do such a thing. Selah †

In this world, people credit the wife when her husband does good and vice versa. But in the eyes of God, each individual is credited with their own works. Selah †

Roger and I have been married for 30 years. When you're married that long EVERY inch of jealousy is gone; especially when the Holy Spirit lives within you. Roger is VERY social with everyone—male and female. He always been that way. As a matter of truth, that's what impressed me about him. He just wasn't respectful to me, but also ALL women. I then knew respectfulness was in him and he wasn't just trying to win me over just by being respectful. Over the years, there have been MANY women, especially women of God, who thought I may be jealous of Roger talking or dealing directly with them. This is far from the TRUTH. Besides, to be honest, I'm the only woman who is anointed and appointed by God to live with and deal with Roger. Therefore, dear hearts, you don't need to come through me to speak to Roger. He's a mature man of God who can talk for himself. Besides I'm the only apple of his eye; of course, after Christ Jesus. Selah †

It's a pure shame when a woman know she has a spirit husband and refuse to be delivered from it; and then a human man connects with her and all hell breaks out. Such relationships end in fatalities. Selah †

Husbands, if your pastor or any man speak to you about your wife and it does not increase your love for her, you need to rebuke those words right in his face. IF not, it will leave a tiny seed planted in your heart; and eventually, it will spring up and be fatal to your marriage. Selah †

A woman wanted deliverance due to having MANY problems in life. She also wanted deliverance for her unsaved fiancé of 11 years. I asked why they're not married and she told me. I then said, "That's not a reason. That's an excuse. His plan is to never marry you." Then I said, "You're not having sex are you?" She then said, "I'm not going to lie to the woman of God. Yes, we are." I then said, "I already knew you were. I just word it that way so you can confess to it. The LORD cannot forgive you unless you first confess to your wrongdoings." Selah †

I had the privilege of ministering deliverance to both husband and wife. After their deliverance, the LORD instructed them to minister deliverance to their children (ages 8 – 21). Dear Hearts, if we fear ministering deliverance to our own child, why do you think devils will leave when you minster deliverance to someone else child? Get YOUR family right and then you can CLEARLY see how to get other families right. Selah †

I use to wonder why my friend's husband did not like me. I never done him any wrong. After so many years, I know the answer. Her husband use to be a Muslim and Muslims truly believe all women should be silent at all times. Well, when I met Jesus I cannot keep silent. I'm always talking about Him. And this made that Anti-Christ spirit in him very angry whenever I mention the name Jesus and spoke on His Goodness. This man needed deliverance and did not realize it. Months later he left his wife and still think nothing is wrong with him because he's a minister of the Gospel. Today, there are MANY men like him. Selah †

Don't you know that some husbands are naggers just as some wives? Remember, nagging is an evil spirit. Selah †

Satan will set you up to mess you up. Again, the LORD our God does not use Facebook or any other social media to form a relationship. Facebook serves as a veil and the veil was torn down when Jesus Christ died and rose again. Forming relationships via Facebook is not wise and dangerous. You don't know what you're getting until you have wrapped and tied your emotions into the person. Ask yourself? Would our loving God connect you to darkness? Would He connect you to an individual who have yield their members for devils use? Would He connect you to an individual that will draw you away from Him? Of course, He would not. Therefore, stop looking for LOVE in the wrong place! He can be found right where you are. Seek a deeper relationship with Christ Jesus and He know what you need and will provide it in His time. Selah †

Especially being a child of God, when you're engaged to be married, you cannot act as though you're already married. Even if you have already been sexual active with one another, you still cannot act as though you're married. You cannot do the things married couples do. So hands and lips off and wait until you're married. Selah †

SELAH † THINK ABOUT IT!

Sometimes, wives can be very foolish! Not EVERY woman want your husband. Your husband may be ALL THAT to you, but it doesn't mean he's ALL THAT to me. In times past, the pastor's wife thought I wanted her husband just because we enjoyed Kingdom conversations. Such attitude TRULY reflects lack of spiritual maturity. GROW UP in Jesus' mighty name. Selah †

It's GREAT when both parties seek God for deliverance BEFORE marriage. Such marriages will last because they choose the right foundation and builder. Therefore, don't allow those who refused the correct foundation and builder to discourage you in your marriage. Selah †

Husbands, if you're not strong enough to handle it, don't accept Friend requests from every woman. Especially when their true colors reflect in their profile picture. They will turn your heart from God and your wife if you're married. Selah †

If you're a child of God and in a relationship with no intention of marrying the person, my advice is that you end that relationship because you're setting up yourself and the other person for demonic oppression. Selah †

When your spouse says to you, "I HAVE NEVER LOVED YOU!" It really isn't your spouse who is actually saying those words. Its spirit spouse and they are correct. Spirit spouses don't and can't love anybody! So the next time your spouse say such words, know that it is not your human spouse. Instead of fighting against flesh and blood whom you see, fight in the spirit realm by faith and prayer in God against that which cannot be seen with your human eyes. Selah †

It doesn't matter whether you're married or not. Internet sex is NOT of God. Its demon spirits pornography and masturbation and deliverance is needed in Jesus' mighty name! Selah †

EVANGELIST KING

What can of mess is this?!? You meet a man from Nigeria using the veil of Facebook and go to his country to be married. You then return to USA while he stays in Nigeria due to all sorts of reasons why he cannot come with you. You both then get together via video conferencing and have internet sex. Is this really the work of Holy Spirit? Somebody need deliverance in Jesus' mighty name. Selah †

How vulnerable some husbands are! I was speaking with a husband and he was complaining about things his wife doesn't do. It's to the point that he is no longer intimate with her. I asked him how he feels around other women. He said, "I feel GREAT! They treat me with respect and listen." I then asked, "Do you know why they do that?" He said, "No." I said, "It's because you don't live with them and they don't live with you." Selah †

Satan hates and dislikes the Word of God. He will have a husband disrespect his wife; while at the same time, respect other women. He will have a wife dishonor her husband; while at the same time, honor other men. Remember; it's the LITTLE foxes that spoil the vine. Selah †

Women (of God), you CANNOT live with a man who is not your husband and STILL expect God to be pleased with you. Even the appearance is evil. It is obedience that the LORD God requires and not sacrifices. You can pray and fast all day and every day, the LORD God is not receiving your sacrifices. It is STILL sin in His eyesight. It is so sad that women (of God) think their decision is right and get angry when corrected in LOVE. Selah †

Some husbands are just like Abraham. They don't know when to take heed in listening to their wife. Selah †

Many years ago a woman called me on the telephone. I thought it was strange because this person NEVER calls me. I immediately knew what the LORD God wanted to say to her. So I waited until she asked the question. I was not familiar with the young man in her life. She asked me about marrying him. I knew, by the Holy Spirit, it did not matter what I said, she had made up her mind in marrying him. So I said, "You have already made up your mind in marrying this young man, but the LORD only want you to know what is going to happen to you in that marriage." I continued to say, "Right now you are a very beautiful young lady, but if you marry this man, you will lose that beauty. The way you dress and wear your make-up attracted him; but when you marry him, he will not permit you to dress that way. You will become very depressed and will gain lots of weight and will not look like yourself. When people see you, they will ask whether that is you or not. No matter what I say to you, you are still planning on marrying him." I then asked her if she was going to marry him and she said yes. I then repeated that the LORD knew she was and He only wanted her to know what is going to happen to her in that marriage. She married him and MANY years later, as the LORD said, it happened. When I saw her, I did not recognize her. She was very depressed due to the religious spirit in her husband. As the LORD said, he did not allow her to wear certain clothes and make-up. She dressed like an old hag. Even though they are still together today, she is still going through those things due to the religious spirit in her husband. Dear Hearts, IF and WHEN the LORD God leads me in sharing TRUTH with you, I will not convince you to obey. I will only tell you what the LORD says and leave it up to you whether to obey him. If you choose to disobey or reject Him; don't worry, I will NOT bother you again because in due time, you will see TRUTH. Selah †

Father God did not just give Adam a woman. He gave Adam a wife that was a woman. Selah.

Many people are mistaking lust for love. To prove it, why months or years later they become divorced or separated due to various reasons? The Word says LOVE keep no record of wrongdoings. Selah †

A young girl came to me seeking Godly counsel since she gave her life to Christ Jesus. I lived across the street from her. The women in her church did not counsel her in the way she should go. By the Holy Spirit, I knew about her past life and counseled her in those areas. I also knew her biggest test would come through her former boyfriend and I warned her about that. For the next several days, her faith in the LORD increased. One day as I was going home in a car, my eyes suddenly glanced at her standing on the corner. I immediately saw something strange on her. I was shocked because I had never seen it before; and when I saw it, it looked directly at me. The LORD then said, "It is a demon spirit of fornication. She had sex last night with her former boyfriend." My intention was to not even question her about it; but she immediately came to the house and confessed to what she had done. I counseled her in that area, but she refused to leave the young man alone. She never talked to me again. AGAIN, who you sleep with, you will smell (and look) like. Selah †

I talked with a woman who expressed her concern about her husband toward her weight. He strongly declares his dislike for big women. I then remembered the time after our first child was born. We invited a young couple to our house for dinner. We were talking when the woman's husband changed the subject to big women. He strongly declared how he hate big women and will not have anything to do with them. The wife looked at me and I looked at the wife. She was so ashamed of her husband saying such words because she knew that I had gained 50 pounds during the birth of our child. She also was ashamed because what her husband did not know was a few days before she had called me in tears stressing how love for her husband is dropping due to his weight. Since he was a little boy, he had heart problems and a few years back he received a pacemaker. Due to this problem, he could not gain weight. He was as thin as a pencil; and she complained that during intimate times together by being so thin, she did not enjoy it. As he continued to talk about how he strongly hates big women; I listened to him, I had love for his wife and held my peace in that I did not say what I wanted to say about his weight. Husbands, you may be like this gentleman and you need to realize the same way you feel about the weight of your wife, she may feel the same about your weight. I could have said to this young man, "Yeah. I like my man to have some weight on him. At least I would have something to grab." I was nice and did not say it. Two wrongs don't make a right. It's not the weight of your spouse that matters. You should love them no matter what size they are because you love them. Selah †

SELAH † THINK ABOUT IT!

There are some husbands who withhold their body from their wife. The MAIN reason due to UNFORGIVENESS. The demon spirit unforgiveness constantly remind them of something their wife did or did not do that they did not approve of. Whenever the wife goes to kiss him, he will turn his head. I know many of you are saying that is a spirit wife who is causing that to happen. Spirit wife is there, but it is demon spirit unforgiveness who is keeping the door open for spirit wife. Can you imagine a wife whose husband refuse to be intimate with her since the birth of their seven year old child? Imagine it! It happens; and until the spouse confesses to not forgiving their husband or wife for one reason or another, demon spirit unforgiveness and spirit spouse will not leave. Selah †

You will actually be surprised to know that there are MANY husbands (in God's house) who in the home mistreat their wife. God knows it and He will tell it. Selah †

Some women have such a strong desire to be married, they will accept having another woman's leftover—only to find out later, how stale it is. Selah †

The devil also uses one stone to kill two birds. He will use the stone of UNFAITHFULNESS to get a husband or wife to leave their spouse; and then the husband or wife will leave God. Selah †

The young women of today can be foolish. They allow "no good" men to drive their car and live off of them. When the man get tired of them, they leave to find another woman. Oh, foolish woman! Selah †

Dear Hearts, you CANNOT say a man or woman belongs to you when they are not your spouse. You CANNOT say another man or woman stole your man or woman when they are not your spouse. IF you are not married to that person, they are LEGALLY for grabs. Selah †

Married folks! We need to REMEMBER the case of Ananias and Sapphira. There was a reason why our LORD wrote their case in His Word. It's a warning to married couples. IF our spouse is not giving ear to the Holy Spirit, then we must not give ear to them. Follow them as they follow Christ Jesus. Just because they are your husband or wife does not mean Satan will not mislead you through them. Selah †

Some say, "My husband left me for another woman." Or "My wife left me for another man." What they don't know is that their husband or wife had left them for another partner that COULD NOT be seen with human eyes BEFORE they left them to be with their human partner. When they return, not only should you be concerned about them abandoning the human partner; most importantly, also the partner not seen with human eyes. Deliverance is needed in Jesus' name. Selah †

There was a woman who husband had left her. She called for prayer and instruction regarding how to deal with the situation. From experience, I told her to KEEP her focus and attention on Jesus Christ, which includes doing things to PLEASE the LORD God. About several weeks later, she notified us to let us know that he had returned. My husband then shared a word of the LORD with her for her to share with her husband. Her response reflected that she did not want to say anything that will upset him due to him leaving again. My husband and I felt sorrow for her. A few weeks later, we received a message that when she came home, he had his lawyer present for her to sign divorce papers. Dear Hearts, as God's Word says, when we seek to save our life, we will lose it. This woman thought she was saving her marriage by pleasing her husband in not speaking truth, but she lost it. Selah †

When I was a sinner, there were some things I just REFUSED to do. One of them was getting involved with a married man. It didn't matter to me if he was separated or about to get a divorce, I STILL refused to be involved with him. I had come from a broken home and lived without a father; therefore, I did not want to be held responsible for breaking up nobody's home. Who knows? If marriage-breakers never got involved with separated or divorced couples, maybe those couple would have gotten back together. I ALWAYS remembered God's Word, "You reap what you sow." I felt if I had any measure of causing the breakage of a marriage, then the LORD God would not bless my marriage to last. Selah †

A woman claimed the LORD showed her the man she supposed to marry. She was adamant about him being her husband. To her amazement, she saw the man at her church in the parking lot. She later found out that the man was married and temporarily separated from his wife. Still believing that it was the LORD who showed him to her, she joined a telephone prayer line and asked everyone to pray for her and the man. Everyone then prayed for and with her on the phone. She asked one lady to join her privately for prayer. The lady then said the woman asked her to pray along with her in that the LORD will break up the man's marriage so that he could marry her since the LORD told her he was her husband. The lady REFUSED. Dear Hearts, every time you hear a voice or have a dream, it doesn't mean it is from God Almighty. IF it is the LORD, then the voice you hear and the dream you have will ALWAYS AGREE with His written word. When it comes to a spouse, the LORD God will NOT connect or join us to someone who is not serving Him with all their heart because Light has no fellowship with darkness and He doesn't want us to be unequally bound together. Can you image two being bound together unequally? It's like two oxen when one is strong and the other is a weakling. I'm pretty sure the strong one will drag the weakling until the weakling stop the strong one. Selah †

A young lady called me for help. She was dissatisfied with her husband after being married little over a year. As she shared her concerns I saw their reason for marriage led to their downfall. She married him for security and he married her for "legal" sex. She wanted me to agree with her in leaving her husband, but I would not. Instead I advised her to treat her husband as Christ Jesus has instructed. Regardless of how he treated her, she MUST treat him as a loving wife. Of course, she did not want to hear those words and I knew by the Holy Spirit that she was rejecting them. Then I shared with her what would happen IF she did not obey the LORD's instructions. Since she married her husband strictly for "security", the thing that she loved the most (their house), they would lose it. She really got angry with me and I never heard from her again. Several months later, the friend who referred her to me called and told me that she had confessed to how she got angry with me; and I was right because they did lose their house and then she left her husband. The saddest part to this story is that the woman is on Facebook looking for husband #3. I'm sure she has found him by now. Selah †

You husbands, likewise, conduct your married lives with understanding. Although your wife may be weaker physically, you should respect her as a fellow-heir of the gift of Life. If you don't, your prayers will be blocked. Selah †

Meeting men and women on Facebook for relationship — blind guide. Selah †

I was once reminiscing over my relationship with my husband. I thought about how much we love each other; and then suddenly the thought came, "With the same measure you both love one another, you both can hate one another." That thought saddened me and I then wondered how two people can be in love and then end up hating each other. It just shows how much we TRULY need to KEEP Jesus Christ the FOCUS in our relationships, especially our marriage, and then we will not be double minded. Selah †

I ministered to a young woman due to failure in relationships. TRUE, she had a spirit spouse and was delivered from it and others. She LOVED the LORD God with ALL her heart. BUT, there was one thing the LORD kept reminding her to do. After many months in us talking to each other; SUDDENLY, she said, "Mrs. King, the father of my son, I got him to love me through witchcraft." Once she CONFESSED to her "dirty little secret", she was TOTALLY set free in Jesus' name. I wonder just how many women (and men) have used some type of witchcraft in getting the man or woman they desire. Deliverance is needed in Jesus' name. Selah †

I was ministering to a husband and wife in their home and as I was talking;

SELAH † THINK ABOUT IT!

I knew the LORD was speaking directly to the wife. I then said, "He is with you." I said it again, but this time, I said, "Lo! I am with you always." As I spoke the word "Lo", I placed a strong emphasis on it. I said it again. And then I brought it to her attention that the LORD said, "Lo! I am with you always." I then mentioned to her about the word "Lo". I told her there is something about that word that strongly lets us know that Jesus is with us; and when I get home, I'm going to look it up. I strongly felt that the word is VERY important. I thought about it and looked it up. It is used to call attention to something or to show wonder or surprise". Selah †

When the Holy Spirit lead you to do something, just do it. You may not know the reason why at the moment, but it will be revealed later. I say that to say this. The LORD God told me to do a video on the subject of "Spirit Husband and Spirit Wife". On October 30th, I received a message from a young lady requesting more information. The LORD then told me to ask her to call me. She called me today and we talked about two hours. At the end of our conversation, she told me about a recurring dream in which she was approached by a person forbidding her to have children. I immediately knew it was a spirit husband. So I began to speak warfare prayers over her and asked her to repeat them. As she was repeating them, she began to choke and cough. I immediately knew that the demon spirit husband was trying not to come out so I then commanded it to come out In Jesus' Name. As I began to confess the words of the LORD over her life, I felt it when she placed the telephone down to run to the bathroom. But I continued to deal with the spirit husband and then it left her. She immediately began to praise the LORD God for setting her free. Dear Hearts, the videos and messages that I post on Facebook are not something I am just posting. They are posted to set you free In Jesus' Name. Be it according to your faith. Selah †

As the LORD once said to me, "No head! It's dead!" Meaning, when the head is cut off, the body dies. Whenever the husband (the head of the home) is not in his proper place, which is in the presence of God, the family suffers. When Adam left the presence of God, his family (at that time, it was only his wife and later, his children) suffered. When we fail to set our affection on the things above, dear hearts, we will suffer. Selah †

EVANGELIST KING

The angels of God surrounded my family when we laid down to sleep in a demon possessed church apartment building many years ago. I woke up to their presence protecting us. They were linked together around us. We were in the middle of them and demons were on the outside of them. I had been telling my husband that evil spirits were in the building. He did not believe me until the day we finally decided to leave. We were downstairs using the church office phone when we heard someone open the front door, walk down the aisle and upstairs. My husband looked at me and I looked at him and said, "Do you believe me now?" We waited for a moment to see if someone would walk down the stairs and nobody did. We later told the pastor who owned the building and he said, "I know. The woman who rented the building before was a witch. I had another church member to stay here and he moved because of that spirit." My husband and I thought, why did you put us here! We later found out they weren't true friends. Selah †

BEWARE of apostles, prophets and pastors that say the one you're married to be not your husband or wife. Behold, this person is your husband or wife. RUN AWAY! RUN FROM THAT CHURCH IN JESUS' MIGHTY NAME! They are false ministers sent out from Hell. Selah †

It's good when husband and wife comes to be delivered from spirit spouses! Join your faith with my faith for their total deliverance tonight in Jesus' mighty name. Selah †

Whenever we sin, our LORD Jesus doesn't "quickly" write us off. He refuses to disown us. Even when we have not yet repented, He still will not write us off. He is ALWAYS willing to forgive and forget. Therefore, He sits and waits for us to come to Him. If we are truly serving HIM, then we will not be so quick to write people off, which is to have nothing to do with them. We will be just as Jesus our Master. We will have a forgiving and caring attitude of heart toward them and wait patiently for them to see the error of their ways. Selah †

I learned MANY years ago not to "preach" to my husband. I'm not his preacher. I'm his wife. Whenever he happens to do something contrary to what God's Word say, then instead of preaching to him, I just tell his Father who happens to be my Father. I would say to our Father, "Would you PLEASE tell your son such-and-such." Dear Hearts, I found this action really works. Selah †

Joseph was a handsome young man and a man to be desired. He was no fool; when temptation came, HE RAN! Flee fornication. Selah †

You CAN'T continue to live with a man or woman as though they are your husband or wife even though you are engaged and STILL expect the LORD God to bless you and expect me to be happy for you. IT IS STILL SIN! It does not matter if you're promised to wed. YOU'RE NOT MARRIED! Selah †

I never hear prophetesses say how they desire to be like Prophetess Anna. They always want to be like Ruth. Selah †

In the latter part of the 90s, in the churches my husband and I visited, we would OFTEN hear the pastor and the church leaders speak on how the woman should behave. They should behave like Sarah, Abraham's wife. Sarah called her husband lord. They spoke MANY sermons in relation to this matter. One day as I was listening to them, I asked the LORD about that and this is the conclusion I came to. I said to myself, "Yes. Sarah did call her husband Abraham her lord. If you want me to call my husband the same, then where are my maid servants? Sarah's lord or husband gave her servants. So where are mines?" Selah †

I know a case right now where a young man "thinks" he is getting a woman from God as his wife. He does not know that the woman who he first met and is in love with is an alternate personality of the woman. The real woman is not who he is in love with. Sadly, this young man is so religious that he will not believe the TRUTH. Selah †

EVANGELIST KING

I once had an international Evangelist I befriended due to the GREAT miracles and healings the LORD God manifested in his ministry. I looked forward each day coming to my News Feed and watching the video clips. The LORD was moving powerfully through him in many countries. One day it occurred to me that I no longer were seeing those videos in my News Feed even though he was still on my friend's list. I wondered what could be the problem as to why the videos stopped. Several days later I received a friend request and noticed his profile picture. I thought, "What's going on? Why does he have two profiles?" I then looked at his first profile and then I noticed the posts have changed. His posts did not reflect the "works" of the God, but only his interest in life. I then as the LORD instructed accepted his second request. I noticed his profile picture in which the woman behind him was touching him as a wife would do her husband. I felt "strange" about that picture. I then sent him a private message as the LORD instructed and merely asked these simple words, "Is there a reason as to why you have two profiles?" Dear hearts, his answer was shocking. He said that he only sent requests to certain of his friends from his first profile. Then he proceeded to tell me what happened. As he was sharing his thoughts with me, I knew he thought that I would agree with him. After he finished, I let him know that I could not agree with his actions. He got so upset with me, that he fussed me out and told me that "his" leaders agree with his actions and it doesn't matter what I say. He then defriended me. Dear hearts, this man of God, left his wife to marry his interpreter due to his wife asking him to slow down in travelling so much so that they could have children. They have been in ministry travelling for over 20 years and have never had a family. He said that his interpreter for 8 years understands him and agree with him in travelling in ministry and she also has planned to divorce her husband. And by the way, his profile photograph was of him and his mistress, not his wife. BE CAREFUL! Every profile picture you see on Facebook of a man and woman "acting" as though they are married; they are not. Selah †

Whether your spouse admits to an affair or not, the love of God in you FORGIVES. Selah †

Satan and his kingdom of darkness "hate" marriage. Marriage was designed by God; and whenever we choose to marry, we are really

SELAH † THINK ABOUT IT!

choosing to honor and respect the LORD. Therefore, Satan and his evil kingdom will HATE any person whenever they choose to marry. My husband and I committed sin before our marriage and I became pregnant. Even though he asked me several months to marry him before we even thought about having sex, I declined due to the "rules" of the church. After we sinned and I became pregnant, I thought about his offer because I did not want my child to grow up without her father. We got married. My heart was already in pain due to committing sexual sins. I was always taught to "wait" until you are married to have sex and failed due to taking my eyes "off" the LORD and placing them onto Roger. THIS IS THE REASON WHY I STRESSED SO HARD FOR A PERSON WHO IS SEEKING TO DO THE RIGHT THINGS THAT THEY KEEP THEIR EYES ON THINGS ABOVE, WHO IS CHRIST JESUS, AND NOT ON THINGS OF THE EARTH. Whenever we fail to do this, we will fall smack into Satan's trap(s). After Roger and I married and the "church" leaders found out about it, they were ANGRY. They were not concerned about me and Roger committing sin before the LORD for having sex before marriage. They were upset that we got MARRIED. After they spoke to us about our choice in getting married, we were dis-fellowshipped and shunned by church members and family who were members. I could not understand why they were so angry that we got married. NOW, I know the truth. The demon spirits in them were the ones angry with us that we decided to repent and sin no more by getting married. This coming April will be 31 years of marriage. MANY of those people (and family) have accused us of marrying simple because I became pregnant; but that was not true—getting pregnant only speeded up my decision because eventually I would have married him. Dear hearts, I share my testimony with you because there are "certain" people reading this right now and you are going through difficult times in relations to relationships. Stop committing sexual sins (from the heart) and KEEP your eyes on the LORD God. If a man or woman TRULY loves you, then they will marry you NOW and not keep making promises to marry you. As long as the evil ones can, they will PREVENT you from choosing to marry because marriage honors the LORD. Selah †

ABOUT THE AUTHOR

Today, Mrs. Terry B. King aka Evangelist King continues to answer the supernatural call of and by God, to do the work of an evangelist through *The Children's Mite*, a ministry of salvation, healing, deliverance and giving, with outreach ministry that includes deliverance and feeding programs, as well as healing and deliverance services. She is Founder and CEO. Gifted with a compassion for the lost and neglected, she strives to share the "Good News" of Christ Jesus with everyone she meets. Understanding the Word of the LORD God through His anointed servants, "The work I'm doing in you, no man will be able to get the glory," she continues to strive to share the "Good News" of her Risen LORD Jesus to a physical and spiritual impoverished world.

Evangelist King has also authored, "The Children's Mite" and "Holy Ghost FIRE Talk (Volume 1)" and several e-books. Check our website at www.thechildrensmite.org for more information. Shalom †

www.ingramcontent.com/pod-product-compliance
Lightning Source LLC
Chambersburg PA
CBHW071308040426
42444CB00009B/1920